organizing magic

Other books by Sandra Felton

Living Organized
Messie No More
Organizing Your Home & Family
Smart Organizing
The Messies Manual
When You Live with a Messie

organizing magic

40 days to a well-ordered home and life

sandra felton

Revell
Grand Rapids, Michigan

© 2006 by Sandra Felton

Published by Fleming H. Revell
a division of Baker Publishing Group
P.O. Box 6287, Grand Rapids, MI 49516-6287
www.revellbooks.com

Second printing, January 2007

Printed in the United States of America

Library of Congress Cataloging-in-Publication Data
Felton, Sandra.
    Organizing magic : 40 days to a well-ordered home and life /
Sandra Felton.
        p.   cm.
    Includes bibliographical references.
    ISBN 10: 0-8007-3099-2 (pbk.)
    ISBN 978-0-8007-3099-4 (pbk.)
    1. Home economics. 2. Organization. 3 Women—Time managment.
    I. Title.
    TX147.F35 2006
    640—dc22   2006004839

The authors of any unattributed quotations are unknown.

Contents

Acknowledgments

Thanks to the following for making this book a reality:

As always, to Ivan, supporter extraordinaire at home and in life. Kisses to you!

To Nanette Holt, remarkable editor and hard worker who strengthened the book with her outlook and experience. Wonderful guidance!

To Lonnie Hull DuPont for her faith and encouragement in moving this book into being at Revell. Many thanks!

To Fleming H. Revell, my publisher for the past quarter of a century. Wow!

Introduction

I have loved magic since childhood. And I know I'm not alone.

Many of us have vivid memories of watching Cinderella, sitting in ashes, sad and in disarray. She never had fun and always worked hard. Even so, she was powerless to improve her condition. (Sounded like me when I looked around my messy house.)

But then we rejoiced when she found the prince who whisked her off to a beautiful castle, where she never had to turn her hand to work again. Wow! Can't beat that!

And who brought about the wonderful transformation? Why, the fairy godmother, of course!

For years I waited for my fairy godmother to show up, wave her magic wand over me, and magically change my mess into glorious order, my frustration into joy.

It never happened. The fairy godmother never came to my house. Nor did the elves who worked for the shoemaker while he slept. Nor did the prince, with the reviving kiss, or any of those other magic, fairy-tale people on whom I had subliminally pinned my hopes.

Then I learned where the magic really is—and it changed my life.

In this book I share with you the organizing basics I learned after long ignoring them, waiting for outside help. The information in each chapter contains a little magic dust. Rightly used, you will find your house being slowly—but surely!—changed into the neat, orderly, elegant, comfortable castle of your dreams. And you will be the princess, more relaxed and unhurried, finally able to enjoy your domain.

But *you* must wave the wand. *You* must sprinkle the magic dust. Don't worry—I'll tell you how, step-by-step, walking you through the transformation that will change your life.

Here's your part: Read each chapter carefully. Zero in on how each can help you improve your situation. Note the steps you need to take to create the solutions that apply to you. Then start waving that wand, your treasure trove of solutions. And watch. The magic will come.

Often in fairy tales, like those about Snow White or Sleeping Beauty, a kiss awakens the princess to her new life. So it is with us.

As you follow the hints, tips, suggestions, and encouragements in these pages, always remember to apply them using the magical kiss of organization:

KISS (keep it super simple)

Say it to yourself, when you're tempted to make things more complicated than they need to be. Whisper it again and again. It's an endless source of organizing magic.

Focus on the few changes that work well for you and do those consistently. You'll be surprised at the change that happens. Now get ready for an enchanting journey with me. Our coach awaits . . .

How to Use This Book

A few useful ideas rightly applied can make a significant change in your life. But it is easy to lose track of them. They tend to drift away unless nailed down on the spot as you read. Here are some suggestions on how to hold on to those ideas that relate to your interests and needs.

1. Underline and write notes in the margin when you see or get an interesting idea. (Unless, of course, this is a borrowed book.)
2. Mark important places you want to remember with a small annotated sticky note so you can find it again easily. This works better than turning down corners.
3. Immediately do the easy step that will make a significant improvement in your life, like calling the phone number that will take you off the calling list of telemarketers.
4. Commit to long-term change where you see the need, such as working to change one bad habit or unproductive behavior. Work on one at a time.
5. Keep a running list of things you need to buy on a sticky note attached to the book so it won't get lost while you read. You can then easily take the note to the store later.
6. Write a to-do list in the back of the book (projects and such) as action ideas occur to you.

Day

Ready, Set, Go!

When I was younger, I embraced many ideas I gleaned from tip books—even the ones that weren't very good. Why? I thought the "expert" who wrote the book was smarter than I was and surely wouldn't lead me wrong. But if I had stuck with all those suggestions, you'd see the following when visiting my house:

- Salmon poached in the dishwasher. It may work, but is it really a good idea to go that quirky route? (Unless your stove is out of order, of course, in which case using this method might make you look like a genius.)
- Nail polish and pantyhose stored in the fridge. They'll keep "fresh" longer there, but do we really want to dress out of our appliances?

- Homemade soap-on-a-rope, created with soap slivers stuffed into the toes of pantyhose.
- Onions kept fresh by suspending them in legs of pantyhose straddling a door.
- Still more discarded pantyhose, recycled as pillow stuffing. (Pantyhose, for some reason, seemed the solution to nearly any household problem.)

I Wised Up

It took me some time to wise up a tad. Now I've learned to avoid introducing things into my life that are far out of the pattern that already exists. If a new idea is not easy to incorporate and easy to follow as a regular part of my life, I

Smart Thinking!

How you think affects how organized you are—and how organized you will become. Try reprogramming yourself to become more organized by meditating for a few minutes daily on these positive statements:

1. **I am too smart to create a mess. Therefore, I put things where they belong immediately after using them.**
2. **I am too smart to let the kids make a mess. Therefore, I spend the time and energy to train them to keep things orderly.**
3. **I am too smart to do everything myself. Therefore, I create a team of family, friends, and hired help to call on when I need assistance.**

reject it. What a relief to have finally found that I don't have to integrate all great ideas into my life—I need only the ones that will make *my* life easier.

In this book you'll find many suggestions, strategies, and tips. Employing well-chosen tips will free up your life—now and for years to come. Happily embrace those.

A few you'll try now and perhaps abandon later. But don't cheat yourself by not trying at least a few new things, even if you're not sure they'll work for you. Some of the ideas I thought originally were the poorest, like grouping my clothes in the closet according to category and color, have proven to be lifelong time-savers. Had I not tried them, despite my doubt, I never would have known!

Sometimes you will see what seem to be contradictions. This is often true with words of advice. Tradition tells us that you can't tell a book by its cover. Yet we're also admonished that first impressions are the most important. We're told to look before you leap. But we're also warned that he who hesitates is lost. Which of the truths in each pair is correct? Both are—but they apply in different circumstances. For instance, sometimes you should be impatient with clutter and take bold steps to move forward. At other times you need to be patient when it comes to moving forward, even when you become discouraged with how slow the improvement seems.

Never fear. I'll help you sort out how to tell the difference.

I define organizing as doing something smart—proactively—to make life easier and more productive. That may include setting up an organizational plan such as the Messies Anonymous Flipper, found at www.messies.com. Perhaps it's making a chore chart for your children. It may be clearing out the house, so there isn't as much to dust. It may be giving up some less important responsibilities, so you can narrow your focus on more significant areas of your life.

What Do Tips Have to Do with It?

The purpose of this book is not to ratchet up the details of your life a notch or two. It's not designed to help you fly higher and longer, to be more of a hardworking perfectionist. You're probably already expending most of your time and energy and don't want to expend any more.

This book will help you work less and still accomplish your aims—maybe even better than before and certainly more efficiently. As you read, you'll see tips that will work for you, helping you simplify what you do and how you do it. These tips are proven strategies for getting and staying organized.

Some tips require time and energy—for you, they may take more effort than they're worth. You may have already tried and rejected some of my suggestions. But keep an open mind. You may decide that tips you once knew and have forgotten, or had earlier rejected, may be useful to you now.

Does this book cover all of the tips and strategies you will ever need? Unlikely. But I *can* promise you this: if you follow appropriate tips in this book, your organizational life will improve significantly. You will be amazed.

So how do you know when to use a tip? Listen to your instincts and your emotions.

Some tips will meet an immediate need. Some will provide a great solution for the future. Ignore the ones that will never be useful for you. Each tip is designed to help you find order and beauty in your life. And like tools, they require intelligent handling to work well.

> **There are no shortcuts to any place worth going.**
> Beverly Sills, opera singer

Your education won't stop here. I warmly invite you to join us daily at www.messies.com. It will provide a springboard into a whole ocean of help from people struggling with, and overcoming, the same problems you're facing.

Forty Days to Fabulous

There are forty chapters in this book, all designed to help you radically improve your life in forty days—just maybe not consecutively. What I mean is this: to make this book work for you, you need to pace yourself. You may be tempted to race ahead, reading more than one chapter a day. But that won't give you the time you need to really put the tips in place.

I'm not suggesting you drag your feet. But we're aiming for big changes. Some chapters involve simply learning to see solutions in a new way. With those your progress will likely be immediate. But the solutions in other chapters may take some time to set up. Don't feel as though you've failed if you halt for a day or two and take time to fully implement tips from those chapters before moving on to the next.

Above all, know that you're not alone. I'm still smoothing out the rough spots that crop up in my own life, even after being known for decades as The Organizer Lady.

So, welcome! I'm so glad to have you coming along with me on this journey.

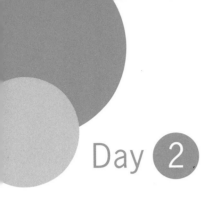

Day 2

Envision Your Goals

It's time to get excited about what your house can be. Frustration may have started you on the road to change, but excitement will take you even farther than you ever dreamed you could go.

Bring That Dream into Focus

You can't go in your everyday life where you haven't gone in your dreams. When you start daydreaming in detail, it becomes planning.

You can stimulate your dreaming by looking around at the lives of friends you admire, the ones who really seem to have their act together. Think back on how Mom did things, if that's the life you want for

> I want peace. I want to see if somewhere there isn't something left in life of charm and grace.
>
> Rhett Butler, in the movie
> *Gone with the Wind*

yourself. Read decorating magazines. Visit model homes or open houses. See, feel, smell what you want your house to be.

Read over the statements below and spend a moment thinking about each. Check those that apply to you. You may even have your own to add.

___ I want to be happy when I step into my house.

___ I want my home to reflect my personality and my style.

___ I want my home to be a good launching pad for my family and me.

___ I want to be free from the stress that clutter causes.

___ I want to use my house to meet the needs of others.

___ I want to be able to find things easily.

___ I want to spend less time struggling to stay organized.

___ I want my house to be beautiful.

___ I want a place to train my kids to be responsible, organized adults.

___ I want _____.

___ I want _____.

The Big One

It is your pleasure, your privilege, your high calling, to set goals, to envision a dream. Make it a big one. *The* Big One.

Nothing short of bold vision will be enough to propel you to create the home you envision for your family and to maintain it that way in the years to come. Let me say *for* you what you

This book is about
defining your dream
and setting a pace
to pursue it.

may not have the boldness to say for yourself: "I want a house that is beautiful, clean, even shining. I want it to be neat and tidy and *stay* neat and tidy. I want to welcome unexpected guests with joy, because I can bless them with the atmosphere of my home, and I can meet their needs there. Houseguests will share themselves with us, and we with them, in the comfort of our house.

"I want . . . no, I *need* a house that is easy to live in. It supports me in what I do because things are easy to find and easy to get to. I don't have to struggle to move forward in my projects in this house.

"My family is proud of our home—so proud that they want to be part of keeping it clean and in order. Their friends are welcomed, and they enjoy what we have to offer them here.

"My habits and their habits keep the house nice—consistently—not perfectly but consistently. I want to feel in control of my belongings, papers, and finances, so that area of my life does not become chaotic, frustrating, and even scary. I work smoothly—without wearing myself out in this quest—because I have developed a system that works.

"The words *dignity, serenity,* and *harmony* are not strangers in my house. Is it dusty from time to time, or are there things out of place? Perhaps. But never so much that the integrity of what I, or we, have created is lost.

"This is not just a house. I will not be satisfied until I have fully created a true home, with *all* that word embodies. I know that specific strategies, tips, and steps toward order are important, because they are the nails that hold together the boards of this dream."

This book is about defining your dream and setting a pace to pursue it.

What is the allure of marathons? There are many, I'm sure. But for most, I think, it's the challenge of doing something you thought you could never do. When you do it, what a thrill!

> **Order is the shape upon which beauty depends.**
>
> Pearl S. Buck,
> author and winner of the
> Pulitzer Prize and Nobel Prize

This book will help you make a commitment to your dream, challenge yourself to new heights, and upgrade your house and life in a way that may seem impossible now. Take it day by day, slowly and steadily. You will be thrilled when you cross the finish line of your desires.

Do Just a Little Better

I won't bore you with the cliché of a journey beginning with just one step, though I'm tempted to do so, because it's so true—especially in this context. In housekeeping, truly, just a few little changes can make a huge difference.

Often careless or casual habits just need to be upgraded a little bit. Usually the difference between good and great is just a little more effort, just one more step.

If you find yourself being too relaxed about something, simply decide to ratchet up your effort a notch next time. Then make that upgrade a habit.

Below is one example of something we all do—buy a new multipack of toilet paper. The question is, what do we do with it? This is a task we handle at different levels of organization. Take the famous Felton Toilet Paper Test. Which level are you on?

- Leave it in the car until needed (or nearly needed, I trust!).

- Bring in the package and drop it in the kitchen or by the back door.
- Put the still-wrapped package in a bathroom.
- Remove the rolls from the package and put them all in one bathroom.
- Distribute toilet paper to all bathrooms, so it will be easily available when needed.
- Slip them under cute, little decorative covers, stashed close to the toilet.

Wouldn't it be easy to jump up one level at least? The importance of upgrading is this: your needs will be met with greater ease. Certainly having toilet paper readily and consistently available relieves stress, saves time, and keeps the household moving along without unnecessary effort.

Stop, Start, Continue

To put feet to your goals and start moving ahead, you must realize that reaching a goal requires behavior change. Have you thought recently about the behaviors that get in the way of your dreams, or about the habits you must initiate to get where you want to go? It's time to evaluate them, decide how to deal with them, and move forward.

Make three columns on a sheet of paper, labeling them *Stop, Start, Continue*.

In the first column, write three habits you want to stop because they are hindering your journey toward your dream. Maybe you will write, "Watching late-night TV every night," because you know it zaps your energy the next day, or "Serv-

> **A year from now you may wish you had started today.**
>
> Karen Lamb, author

ing as president in my club," because it takes up more time than you have to give.

Under the second heading, list habits you intend to start. They may be things like, "Make lunches every night," or "Do one load of laundry each day," or "Hire help."

> **Conduct is influenced, not by our experience, but by our expectations.**
>
> George Bernard Shaw, British playwright and novelist

Behaviors to continue are those that are useful and successful in your life, like "Continue painting regularly," or "Continue walking each morning."

For this to work, under each heading you'll need to list three or more behaviors. Writing your planned behaviors and reviewing the written goals daily will dramatically increase your chances of sticking to them, research shows.

This is amazingly simple. Will you do it and adjust your life in the direction of your dream by stopping what hinders it, starting what advances it, and continuing the good stuff? I know you can!

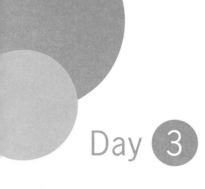

Party Your Way
to Order and Beauty

Constantly zeroing in on the problem of disorder in the house can be a real drag. Focusing on overcoming problems is important, but the best motivator is working for a fun, worthwhile goal like (drumroll, please) throwing a party!

As I See It

As I struggled to gain control of the condition of my house, I realized one day that there's more to this building than just a dwelling, a launching point into the world. It isn't just a laundry, dressing room, snack bar, place to sleep, or place my family and I depend on to launch us into the real world.

I'd gotten it backwards. The outside is not the real world. Our house *is* the real world. The outside world existed to support what happened inside the *house*!

In truth, the home is a womb where relationships between family members and with friends are nurtured. Often the home is the wellspring of ministry and nurturing others. Sometimes it's a place of business. Always it should offer relief to the people who live there—to you and me and the loved ones who share the home with us.

> To invite someone into our home creates a bond like nothing else can.

Life outside the home is sometimes difficult. We can't control all that happens there, but we can create a soft place to fall within our four walls.

So Much to Celebrate

Despite chaos in our jobs, on the crowded streets, or in bustling stores, the home is the one place we can create serenity and harmony. And one way we can celebrate this fact is by entertaining there.

We can eat with friends at restaurants, but it's not nearly as personal and meaningful—for them or for us—as when we open our home and share ourselves in our own unique context. To invite someone into our home creates a bond like nothing else can.

Yes, it can be scary! Is the house nice enough? Is it neat enough? Is it clean enough? Is it pretty enough? Am I good enough? Many of us bombard the notion of having people over with a cruel barrage of self-doubt.

The result? We keep other people away—away from our homes and away from our very souls. Why? A relationship that becomes personal may lead to visits from home to home. So to avoid the stress of entertaining or the explanations of why no invitations have been extended, many of us remain just aloof enough to avoid that kind of dilemma.

Maybe, as I once did, you've kept people at arm's length for so long, you can't even think of a friend close enough to invite over. What a shame!

Often people with this problem are loving and outgoing people, but they don't want to risk developing and enjoying friendships because of (say this as if you're in an echo chamber) "THE HOUSE."

If you are one who doesn't want to live with this kind of tension anymore, start by slowly developing deeper friendships. After keeping people out of your home for so long, you'll feel more comfortable if you ease slowly into a more welcoming lifestyle. To begin, try inviting someone in "for just a minute" while you get your coat on or grab your purse.

Though it's hard to break old molds, the rewards are great: Nothing else meets the inner needs of the soul like positive relationships. Your home can express your personality at its best. And knowing that someone will be coming to your home will propel you to maintain it in a way that's more pleasing for you and your family.

Ready to claim these benefits for your own? Face the fear and resolve to just do the following:

- Get the house in "good enough" shape to invite someone in. If the task seems too monumental, just straighten the areas your guest will see.
- Choose your comfort level of entertaining. Maybe it will be a neighbor for coffee and a muffin (maybe even without the muffin).
- Keep inviting one or two people into your home (the same ones or a variety) while you build up to bigger things.

- As your comfort grows and your house is more in order, invite larger groups, like a book club or Bible study. You can still close the doors to the bedrooms, even though more of your house will be exposed.
- Graduate to a real party, free of the worry that guests will get off the beaten path and into every area of your home. Now it all feels "good enough."

Sure, you may be saying, with a furrowed brow, "Easy for you to say. How can I actually do this?"

I'll tell you.

- *Gather serving pieces that make you comfortable.* After years of not having people over, your plates, cups, and flatware may be too shabby to show, and you are simply not prepared to entertain. But that's okay. Even plastic and paper works well too. One lady I know has a hot cider party each Christmas and asks guests to bring their own mugs. It works, and it's charming!
- *Bring guest areas up to par.* Does your guest bathroom need fresh hand towels or a spruced-up soap dispenser? No need to go overboard. Just hit the high spots that need refreshing. The house doesn't have to be a showplace—just comfortable and inviting!
- *Extend an invitation.* Choose someone you feel comfortable with and who has been friendly to you, so you'll feel most at ease.
- *Plan easy-to-serve refreshments.* What you offer your guests doesn't have to be homemade or fancy. You might even allow guests to bring their favorites if they ask what they can bring.
- *Create conversation starters.* If you have one or two friends over, talk about a mutual interest, ask for their advice

on a specific issue (like which accessories go with a new outfit), or show a family album (don't overdo this one unless you know your guests like this kind of thing). For larger groups, you'll have no need to fear a lag in the festivities if you focus your guests' attention on a fun activity, such as asking them to take pictures using disposable cameras or starting a mixer that will encourage them to get to know each other. Find ideas on the Internet by typing "party games" into your favorite search engine.

- *Stop seeking perfection.* Relax and have fun, even if you notice a cobweb hanging from a corner during the gathering. Who cares? Cut yourself some slack. You're a novice at entertaining, and it will get even smoother as you practice having more people over.

I feel sure that you have something special to contribute, and this is your time to do it. Open the door of your life, as far as you are comfortable. Then slowly open it wider as your courage grows and your house seems more acceptable to you.

Friends, fun, and fellowship are important. And in these get-togethers you're about to organize, they're all that matter. Really.

Your house is just the canvas. The masterpiece—a work in progress—is the pleasing mix of relationships you build in it.

You have a special song to sing. Don't go any longer without belting out that melody to the world with gusto.

Day 4

Be Annoyed— Very, Very Annoyed

There are two reasons people take the trouble to change how they live. The first is a desire for harmony. These people simply want to live more beautifully and peacefully.

Others, however, seek change as a desperate attempt to relieve the discomfort of disorganization and the pain of clutter. They're powerfully motivated to do what it takes to end the frustration they feel.

Good Reasons to Be Annoyed

That said, go ahead and be annoyed. It's okay. It's even desirable. Be very, very annoyed when

> **Failure usually comes in many small steps, not through one giant leap. Success is the same way.**

- You can't find your tax information. But you have no choice—you have to search doggedly for the lost papers.

- You need to mail a letter but don't have a stamp. So you put the letter aside, hoping you'll remember where you put it when you finally buy stamps. In the meantime, the letter becomes hopelessly lost.

- The new lightbulb you need is stored high on a shelf behind a precariously balanced pile of stuff. Touch it, and everything will tumble. So you put off replacing the burned-out bulb. In the meantime, you strain to see in the dimness.

- You can't find clothes that match. You do the best you can to put together an outfit quickly so you're not late—again.

- You can't invite people into your house because it's just too messy. You learn to live without the companionship you always hoped you'd enjoy in your home. Making excuses to keep people out has become automatic.

- You forget the birthday of your favorite great-aunt, who may not have many more birthdays left. You planned to send her a sweet card, but you don't have a system for remembering these kinds of occasions. Regret over mistakes like this often clouds days that should have been happy.

Tune In to Annoyance

A disorganized life is, at its core, annoying. Maybe you've learned to live with it and have ignored it so often that you

barely notice anymore. Like a
shoe that pinches or the noise on a
busy street near your home, you've
learned to tune it out, to a degree.
But it still hurts.

> **A disorganized life is, at its core, annoying.**

Stop. Don't do this to yourself anymore. Tune in to your negative feelings.
Turn up the volume on them. Let them
bubble to the surface and stay there. Zoom in
on the "little" things that are diminishing the quality of your life.

Simply admitting to yourself how these annoying problems make you feel is the first big step toward solving them.
Really.

Let the irritation energize you. Let it propel you toward
finding a solution that works—one that sends your old friend
annoyance packing. Ahhhh, it feels so good to get that rock
out of the shoe!

Take Better Care of Yourself

Disorganization is a problem of self-neglect. In short, when
we're disorganized, we're failing to treat ourselves with the
love and respect we want others to show us.

By becoming more organized, we become more powerful
in taking care of ourselves. And here's an important payoff:
when we take care of ourselves, we take better care of those
around us as well.

But it's challenging to keep modern life organized. These
days life runs on so many different tracks that if we're not careful, parts of what's important to our well-being can derail.

Getting dressed in the morning is a hassle when you can't
find the right blouse, jewelry, or shoes. Because you're late,

> **Winners make it happen.
> Losers let it happen.**

you don't have time to fix a proper lunch to take to work. You become so frazzled that you forget to write a note to buy moisturizer. You realize you just incurred a late fee because a bill you've been meaning to pay is now overdue. You can't have friends over because of how the house looks. One small derailment after another adds up to self-neglect.

What's more, when you're so muddled in your own life, you neglect your responsibilities to others. You can't find and sign your child's school papers. Dinner is a last-minute affair—no choice but to order in pizza (again!). Finances unravel, so you hesitate to buy what is necessary.

Being disorganized is a disservice to those you love and to you. Becoming well organized is an important gift you give yourself—and others.

Day **5**

Learn the Secrets of Organizing Magic

When it comes right down to it, I think people are divided into two groups. The first is made up of those mystifying folks who are efficient without seeming to work at it. Their living rooms always are ready for unexpected guests—maybe not perfect but acceptable. When they step back into the kitchen to clean up after a meal, very little needs to be done. Their laundry is kept up. All of this seems to be done mysteriously without much effort. Those of us who wrestle with chaos look on with amazement. How do they do it?

Like exposing a magician's secrets, I am now about to reveal how they are so organized.

Taking Few Steps

Organized people automatically keep things neat as they go. That's their goal. For example, your organized friend pours

Make this your family's new motto: If you get it out, put it back quickly.

a cup of coffee. She tears open the artificial sweetener package and flips open the trash can lid with her foot while depositing the empty packet. In one motion, she grabs and pours the powdered creamer, and without putting the jar down, returns it to the cabinet—coffee, with no mess to clean up, no work.

Her less-organized friend (I will insert my name here) has only one goal in mind—a cup of hot coffee. She pours the coffee and adds the sweetener, dropping the empty or half-empty packet on the counter. She adds her creamer and sets the jar on the counter too. Even if she stops now to put things away (highly unlikely!), she's created two extra steps, and those few extra steps during the day really add up. But more

Slash the Work by Saving Steps!

You can save steps and beat clutter by building these habits into your daily routine:

- Toss messy spoons into the sink or dishwasher rather than leaving them on the counter.
- Toss clothes directly into the hamper as you take them off.
- Carry cleaning products in a bucket that travels with you from room to room. When you're finished, simply put the bucket away.

likely, she plans to straighten up later. She sits down while the coffee is hot, leaving a trail of clutter, including a few grains of sweetener dribbling from the packet—more mess on the counter, more work.

You'll save so much time and effort if you just make this your family's new motto: If you get it out, put it back quickly.

Fixing It Quickly

The difference between people who maintain order consistently and those who have to go back constantly and straighten up messy areas is this: orderly folks hop quickly to a solution when something needs to be done. Simply put, as soon as there is a job to do, they do it. You'll keep chaos under control too if you get in the habit of tackling jobs quickly.

- Unload the dishwasher when the load is finished.
- Empty the dryer, fold clothes, and put them away immediately.
- Insist that kids put away toys they're no longer using before dragging out new ones.

Pursuing Consistency

The system you choose to use is not as important as how you work it. Any system, no matter how simple or inadequate, that is consistently worked is better than the best system that's used inconsistently. This is a bold statement but true.

One of the characteristics that sets organized people apart from those who find themselves slipping into disorder easily (often without the slightest idea of why) is that they work in a routine kind of way. They get in a groove of staying on top of the basics and—voila!—they seem to have an organized house with little effort. But don't let them fool you into thinking they don't work at it. They just work efficiently because they're consistent, and that's what makes things go more smoothly.

Not Allowing Ooze

"Oozing" is when things don't make it to their designated area. Keys are not hung on their hook by the door. A wallet is left on the kitchen counter. A cup is forgotten in the living

Stay on Top of the Basics

Slide simple routines like these into your daily activities, and—poof!—your house will suddenly be transformed.

- **Make the bed when you get out of it.**
- **Clean the kitchen before you sit down after a meal.**
- **Put away your toothbrush, toothpaste, and makeup before you leave the bathroom to start your day.**

room, and a jacket is draped on the back of a kitchen chair. When things ooze out into the open where they don't belong, the peace of your home is compromised.

> It is much better to *keep up* than to *catch up.*

But we ooze away from home too. In hotel rooms, things start spreading out of suitcases. Clothes ooze into the room if not corralled into the closet, drawers, or suitcase. In the bathroom, toiletries lie scattered across the counter instead of being lined up neatly along the vanity. Neat people value the pleasure and convenience of order wherever they are.

Ousting Ooze

When your house looks junky and you can't find things, you are probably oozing. But you can oust ooze forever if you simply

- Get in the habit of putting things away as soon as you're finished with them.
- Make a pickup sweep of the house before dinner and before bedtime. Hint: Stay-at-home moms need to add regular toy sweeps too.
- Think like a sheepdog. Constantly nudge your wayward "sheep" (belongings) back to where they belong in the sheep pen. Better yet, don't let them stray at all.

Being Visually Alert

An awareness of how things look is a powerful help when keeping things organized. It

> Every minute you procrastinate putting something back where it belongs is a cluttered minute.

sounds obvious, but some people can't really "see" the clutter. While some people automatically notice when things are out of place, others seem to tune out the mess. They tune in visually only for short intervals from time to time.

But the act of being visually alert is powerful. Try it, and, well, you'll "see." Focus on the condition of your surroundings. The more you do it, the neater your house will stay.

Here's a trick that will allow you to view your house, and its condition, with fresh eyes. Just turn on all the lights at night, open the blinds and drapes wide, and stand outside, like a stranger looking in. What do you see?

Inside, hold an empty toilet tissue or paper towel roll to one eye, like a spyglass. Then look at your kitchen counter, dining room table, or any clutter spot. Take note of which areas seem orderly and which don't.

As you sensitize yourself visually, you will begin to be aware of the reward in putting things away quickly and consistently. The more beautiful and orderly your house becomes, the more zealous you'll become to maintain it that way. The big, really big, payoff comes when your friends begin to say how nice your house looks. Whoopee!

Day

Cooperate with Your Personality Style

You have a wonderfully unique personality. Part of that uniqueness is your organizational style and how you function.

Organizational Style

Most of us use a combination of several styles, but we lean most heavily on one or two that work best for us. Any style that moves you forward is a good one.

When it comes to getting things done, most of us fit one of these five styles:

> *The Planner.* You have developed a basic strategy to make sure life moves smoothly, and you follow those steps. A master plan and calendar are important tools for you. You've tweaked the basic routine to fit your lifestyle,

and that keeps you from having to reevaluate every day and every week to know what to do.

The Delegator. As much as possible, you appoint or hire others to help bear the load. In a way, you are a manager. A good manager is a wonderful thing. Not only do things get done efficiently, but the team (family) learns to work together and the children are trained for adult life.

The Lister. You make lists that dictate your daily and weekly activities. You may create lists for nearly every facet of your life. I know people who write a list and set about doing the items on the list with an impersonal attitude. Zip, zip, zip, they do one job after another, making steady progress and getting things done.

The Vigilant One. You follow the all-the-time-on-top-of-things approach, rapidly completing a task shortly after it presents itself. People with this style seldom put things on a list, because as soon as they see something that needs doing, they hop to it. They often follow a mental list unconsciously.

The Worker. You put in long hours of hard work—a good quality when balanced with qualities of the other styles. You need to remember to take breaks and rest to "sharpen your ax."

The Focuser. No matter which of the other styles you use, everyone needs to be a focuser first and foremost. The focuser prioritizes well and handles the important things efficiently. A focuser is not distracted by the unimportant.

If you allow the unimportant tasks to swallow up your time, your life will be strangely unproductive, no matter how hard you work. But if you're focused, emphasizing only the few important things in your life and what supports their moving forward,

you'll be amazed by your progress. And when you're focused,
your basic style—no matter
what it is—can be a great tool
in organizing your life.

Determine Which Style Works Best for You

I'm not one to keep on top of everything, nor am I one who
follows a list in a mechanical way. I'd best be described as a
strong focuser.

My style does involve making lists of things to do so they
won't drift off my mental radar screen. So, referring to my list,
I gather the materials, information, or whatever is required
to move forward. I observe the time. Then suddenly I get the
urge to do the job. Using a touch of spontaneity, like a spider
that feels an insect hit her web, I jump into action.

Becoming aware of my own style helps me keep my priorities in mind, and I seem to accomplish a lot. If I tried to force
myself to use other, "better" methods, which are not my style,
I would end up doing very little, I suspect. Then I would berate
myself for procrastination and laziness.

So here's the key. Tune in to what works best for you. Use
that method as your main approach for getting things done.
Sometimes you may switch to one of the other ways of ap-
proaching tasks, or you may use a combination. Whichever
approach you take, make sure you *just do it*.

Basic Retraining

Some basic styles siphon the power right out of decision making, throwing us out of focus and truly offtrack. You'll find you're

> Until you make peace with who you are, you'll never be content with what you have.
>
> Doris Mortman, author

much more productive—and, as a result, more relaxed and able to provide a better environment for yourself and your family—if you ease away from employing these basic styles:

The Free Spirit. Doing what is exciting, interesting, or fun are the primary criteria directing your behavior. As a result, much in your life is left undone, causing a ripple effect of disorder and disharmony. Learn to value the dreaded word *discipline.* It is a part of maturity. You'll actually have more fun if you weave it appropriately into your spontaneous life.

The Rusher. Your life is full of demands, and you move spontaneously from activity to activity, hurriedly trying to accomplish much but often sacrificing quality for speed. For you, the word is *focus.* Do less. Tend only to what is really important and stick with it till done.

The Pleaser. You choose activities based on what pleases others and their needs. As a result, you don't accomplish many of the things that are really important in your life. The word you need to focus on is *self-fulfillment.* At first this may seem uncomfortably selfish. But you don't want to neglect the God-given reason for the unique talents you have.

See a lot of yourself in one of these styles? Don't be afraid to change. Modifying a few characteristics like these will not destroy your unique nature. It will enable you to develop the valuable parts of yourself more fully—benefiting not just you but others too. That is a formula for happiness and fulfillment in life.

Day

Battle Boredom
and Lethargy

Often on the Messies Anonymous website, forum participants express that finding the motivation to just get up and do a job that needs to be done is the biggest challenge. After that, the actual tasks seem simple.

Let's face it. For most of us, housekeeping is not an exciting, can't-wait-to-get-started task.

Some people don't seem to mind doing routine tasks. Others, however, can hardly drag themselves to wade through folding a basket of clothes, emptying a dishwasher, or cleaning a toilet. Because these tasks will start coming at us again soon after we accomplish them, for some of us they seem as tedious and pointless as spooning water out of the ocean. Many of us work best only when we're "inspired," and housework rarely rises to that level.

So one undone task after another piles up. Looking at the magnitude of the job, the uninspired person is more listless

43

than before. A recipe for failure is brewing.

An Exciting Antidote

Blast boredom! Eliminate lethargy! They're stumbling blocks that hinder organizing plans, no matter how well intended we are.

Consider the problem of low adrenaline. Having little adrenaline often makes the difference between someone being a go-getter or a slow-getter. But adrenaline can be boosted!

William James, the famous psychologist, says, "Nothing is so fatiguing as the eternal hanging-on of uncompleted tasks." The reverse is true. Here's what I say: Nothing is so exhilarating as finishing up a previously uncompleted task, or to put it more simply: Wow! I did it! I finally did it!

Tricks for Success

By stimulating ourselves with goals, and the happiness of achieving those goals, the downward spiral turns upward. To start that upward spiral, try the following tricks. They will help you become more interested in doing what needs to be done, boring or not.

Put on stimulating music. Polkas, marches, rock, whatever happy music gets your blood (and adrenaline) flowing. Knowing there is an end to the music also encourages you to get the job done quickly.

Make a commitment to complete the job by telling someone your deadline. Maybe they can join with you in a buddy system. Or start an accountability group with several friends. Put money in a winner-takes-all pot that will be forfeited if you don't get the job done. The

pressure of being accountable will stimulate your spirits. Sometimes people call a friend or place a fifteen-minute challenge at an online support group chat room, like the ones at www.messies.com. Promise to get back in touch, either by phone or email, to report how you've done. Then do it!

Change your thinking. Tell yourself that although this part of the job is boring, it's part of a larger and exciting project—transforming your cluttered home into an organized oasis. Still not convinced? Listen to something motivating that will guide you through transforming your thinking. I recommend the audiotape *Create Your Dream and Live It* at www.messies.com.

Reward yourself for finishing the job. Plan to make a special long-distance call, take a friend to lunch, treat yourself to a body splash or piece of costume jewelry, or whatever makes you happy, as a reward for a completed job.

Attach a boring job to something you enjoy. For instance, borrow or buy a book on tape and listen to it only when you're filing, cleaning the kitchen, dusting, or doing whatever boring chore you've been avoiding. You'll be excited to get back to it the next day to see what happens.

Set up an automatic routine that includes the boring job. Commit to a routine of three or four "boring" jobs (like making up the bed, taking out the garbage, handling the mail, and folding laundry) first thing every morning. That eliminates the extra energy drain of having to make a daily decision of when, or if, to do tasks you know need to be done. When you make the commitment, habit takes over and gives a boost. It surprises some people to learn that you can be committed to jobs, not because you like the job itself but because you like the result.

Finally, if possible, get help. Consider hiring someone—a professional house cleaner, a teenager, or a family member—to do some jobs you really despise. The energy and time you save may allow you to focus on something that will provide an even bigger benefit to your family. You may even find that when you work alongside someone else, the job is much easier and less boring.

Recognize the Time Realities of Modern Life

Why are we so rushed and pressed for time? It seems that fifty years ago people had more time for family, hobbies, visiting with friends, even rocking on the porch. They had a general ease of life. Even just decades ago people seemed less stressed and less hurried. What is going wrong?

While we weren't looking at what was slowly happening in society year after year, little time-stealing rascals began sneaking in, ruining our efforts at sensible time management. Now, thanks to a swarm of new inventions and demanding societal changes, no matter how hard we try to simplify, our lives are inexplicably short on time.

But you *can* break free from many of these greedy, modern, time stealers, like:

> A habit cannot be tossed out the window; it must be coaxed down the stairs a step at a time.
>
> Mark Twain

• *Hanging on hold.* Sometimes there is just no way around it. You're afraid to hang up the phone for fear of losing your place in the customer service line. You may have a chance to leave a message, but you're concerned that they won't return your call. Besides, you have all that time invested in the waiting already. Be brave! Leave a message. Better yet, see if the company has a website and send an email to customer service. Then let

Three Ways to Keep Time on Your Side

You can put off your urge to procrastinate if you simply

- *Post action-urging reminders.* In areas where you're often tempted to let chores pile up, place notes such as "Do it now" or "Put these away." Need more encouragement? Add to your little sign the positive consequence for your quick action or an empowering Scripture verse.
- *Commit for a week.* Choose one area of weakness, like making the bed, emptying the dishwasher, or swooping the toothpaste tube back to its proper place. Then vow to do it quickly for a week. After that trial period, consider whether to continue the commitment until a productive habit is cemented.
- *Set deadlines for yourself.* You'll urge yourself to action if you follow through on unpleasant consequences, such as: "If I don't plant this plant this week, I am going to give it away" or "If I don't pay this bill today, I will burn a dollar bill."

your email in-box do the waiting for you.

- *Reading complex owner's manuals.* Most new gizmos come with a quick-start guide that describes all we'll ever need to know.

> **We are what we repeatedly do. Excellence then is not an act, but a habit.**
>
> Aristotle, philosopher
> (384–322 BC)

Don't buy into the warning on the box demanding that you must read the entire manual before using your new time-saving gadget. Glance at it for the parts you need and note the safety info. Usually that demand is more for the company's protection than yours. (Ignore this bit of advice if you are skydiving or handling dynamite.) Just be sure to file the complete guide for reference later.

- *Driving long distances unnecessarily.* If you're driving across town for appointments with your hairstylist, dentist, doctor, or other service providers, consider finding professionals closer to home.

- *Ferrying kids to organized activities.* Instead, strive mightily to do the car pool thing, sharing chauffeuring responsibilities with another adult. Get older, responsible siblings to do some of your driving. Or engage the grandparents if you can. Depending on where you live, older kids may even be able to use public transportation.

- *Having to become a technician.* I never dreamed I would find myself fixing the printer on my computer, hooking up the cordless phone, and trying to solve complex computer glitches. In the "old days," professionals hardwired the phone into the wall and you took a broken appliance to the local fix-

> **A nail is driven out by another nail. Habit is overcome by habit.**
>
> Desiderius Erasmus,
> sixteenth-century philosopher

it shop. Seldom, if ever, was "some assembly required" on things purchased for the house. If you're wasting a lot of time assembling things, stop buying things that need assembly. If you're trying to fix or install mechanical items, consider calling an appropriate professional to do the job for you. The money you spend may actually be a savings in the long run.

- *Watching TV or surfing the Internet for hours.* You'll be amazed at the free time created by turning off the television, the mother of all time wasters, and her sleek, even-more-modern sister, the computer.

Did You Know?

- About 90 percent of children who lived within a mile of their school walked or biked to school in the 1960s. Only 31 percent do so today.
- About 30 percent of morning traffic is caused by parents dropping kids off at school.

Think of your life. What are the time stealers that are carrying away precious minutes from your day? When you added them to your life they

> **Nothing so needs reforming as other people's habits.**
>
> Mark Twain

seemed so innocent and necessary, but now they're working together to leave you time starved. Kick them out, and start living peacefully again!

Day 9

Be Patient with Yourself and the Process

When you're trying to upgrade or change your methods, you are truly a work in progress. You may get a great idea for how to organize something, and it may flop badly. Or you may try something for a while and later think of a better way. Sometimes it requires a lot of patience to get through the process of halting and backing up.

Evolving Methods

For example, I decided to keep a record of the paints used in each room of our house. That way, if I wanted to get more paint for repainting or repair, I would have the information I needed. I had several inventive ideas—in the end, none worked well for me.

My first plan was to tape the brand and color behind the light switch plate. But that made it too troublesome to check.

Then I decided to keep the information on a card in a Rolodex card file under "Paint." That was okay, but later I decided it fit better in the "Household" section of my files.

Don't give up if a method doesn't work. Try others until you find one that fits your style.

I also dipped paint-stirring sticks in the paint, labeled them, and stored them in the utility room, as instructed by Martha Stewart. But having so many methods made it hard to remember which method had the most complete record. As it turned out, I recorded some of the paints using one method and some using another.

A friend of mine puts the leftover paint (probably in a smaller container than the large cans) in a closet or storage area of the room in which it was used. This idea is beautiful in its simplicity.

One time I purchased an impressive time-management notebook, then promptly found it too complex for my needs. I was also afraid of losing it. So I abandoned it for a very small notebook and one piece of paper with telephone numbers on it. I tucked both in my purse and hung a large calendar showing the whole year (from an office supply store) on the back of a door.

Obviously it's better to get one great method and stick with it from the beginning. But if you find yourself flip-flopping for a while, be patient as you search for the method that is best for you. Eventually you'll find one you can live with happily. Just don't give up if one particular method doesn't work. Try others until you find one that fits your style.

Perhaps you have the kind of personality that propels you to change systems just because you enjoy a fresh approach. That's

> **Do not fear the winds of adversity. Remember, a kite rises against the wind rather than with it.**

okay too. If you get bored with one method and desire to try something new, switch methods without feeling guilty or wasteful. Just try to limit fresh starts to no more than absolutely necessary, so you don't lose valuable information or miss a step in the changeover.

Toss Destructive Thoughts

Gail was making every effort to improve the condition of her house. Somehow it wasn't working. She worked hard to tidy and clean consistently. But as she looked around, she found she was doing too much work for too little result. There must be a leak in her system somewhere, she told herself.

Gail was right. The leak was at the source of her efforts—in her own mind! She harbored certain destructive thoughts as she moved around the house. They were the source of her continued frustration and failure.

What were the thoughts that slowed her progress? Read on. These probably will sound familiar:

- *I'll get back to that later.*
- *It's not all that important.*
- *Things don't have to be perfect.*
- *I'm too busy right now.*
- *I'll decide on that when I have more time.*

The truth is, Gail is impatient, and her impatience keeps her house disorganized, despite her effort to tidy it. Eager to be on to the next task, she skips details. And she uses the destructive thoughts to give herself permission to move on, leaving jobs unfinished. Along the path of her hurried efforts, she leaves a trail of uncompleted tasks and clutter.

The solution will not come in a day, but it must come daily.

But Gail—and the rest of us like her—can succeed in her quest to get organized. And the key is far simpler than most would ever imagine. We must simply replace destructive thoughts with action-supporting thoughts like:

- *Do it now!*
- *Never leave it till it's done.*
- *If you get it out, put it back—now, not later!*

True, it's tough to break mental habits. But you can do it. Think about those mechanical gopher heads that are part of the children's arcade game—the ones you bop with a mallet as soon as they pop up. Treat your destructive thoughts the same way. When one pops into your head, bop it as fast as possible with the opposite, action-supporting thought.

With this treatment, those gopher heads will get discouraged and stop appearing. And your home, like Gail's, will take on a new look.

Day **10**

Get Mad at the Mess

Becoming fed up with the junk, the struggle, and the whole insane way of life we have created for ourselves is often what it takes to push us into action.

In my case, when I finally came to the last straw (after many straws that I should not have endured), I was, at last, willing to break old habits, like keeping too many things and procrastinating. It was not until I was angry about what clutter was doing to me that I was able to abandon old traditions and standards that had woven themselves into my identity. It was soul wrenching at first, but it was necessary.

Consider this confession from a self-proclaimed chronic Messie who benefited when she finally decided she'd had enough and wasn't going to take it anymore:

My room, as a teenager, had a clear path from the door to the bed, and that was about it. This pattern repeated in my adult life, and continued after I got married and had my own office in our apartment.

When we moved to a town house with twice the square footage as our apartment, I knew that unless I got my mess under control (both in the house and in my mind), nothing would change.

I'd rationalized over the years that I would clean up and make a trip to the Salvation Army to donate things that were still usable. I had to face reality that I was never going to do that. So I just gritted my teeth and said, I just want this stuff out of my life! So into the trash it went.

I'm sure that in the grand scheme of things nobody starved to death or died of exposure because of my decision. Our new house is much roomier. And because we threw away 75 percent of our possessions when we moved, it's been wonderful having much more open space!

Linda

Good for her! Not only did she discard her possessions, but she surrendered her commitment to donating her things to charity, because it was holding her back. She finally admitted the truth to herself—that donating was never going to happen. Nothing is more freeing than learning to make decisions in the light of cold reality. Linda stepped out of the box of limitations she'd created for herself.

Is donating to charity good? Absolutely! But when Linda finally faced the reality that it was holding her back, she threw caution to the wind and went against her original plan. So again, good for her! And good for you if you face what-

> Do not keep anything in your home that you do not know to be useful or believe to be beautiful.
>
> William Morris,
> nineteenth-century poet
> and philosopher

> **Nothing is more freeing than learning to make decisions in the light of cold reality.**

ever realities are holding *you* back and make the moves necessary to boldly overcome them.

So get mad at those messes. And become less tolerant too.

Here's what I mean. Most of us tolerate living with things we don't like. Think about one now. Are you picturing it? Chances are it falls into one of these categories:

- A gift someone you love gave you, but, well, you know . . .

Ditch Unnecessary Stuff and Feel Better Instantly!

One visitor to the Messies Anonymous website shared this telling observation about her motivation for—and the instant payoff of—getting rid of not-quite-right garments:

"I've been working on thinning out my closet. One rule I'm using is to get rid of anything I don't like.

"It sounds simple, but I have so many things that are a little too big or too small; or I don't really like the color; or they need to be ironed, and I never do it, so they're always wrinkled; or I don't like the neckline; etc.

"I'm always a little less happy with how I look on the days when I wear one of these not-quite-right things. If there's less in the closet, and I like all of it, it's easier to find something to wear, and I'm always happy with how it looks."

Chris

- A "mistake" you bought but feel you should keep because you paid good money for it.

> Space is not something to fill with beauty. Space is beauty.

- Something you no longer enjoy because your tastes have changed.
- Something that doesn't fit you or the space it's in.
- Something that's broken.
- Something purchased in good faith that turned out to be unsuitable for your lifestyle, like a rice cooker, hot dog steamer, or salad chopper.

If you're willing to move the excess out of your life but find it difficult to actually do it, make your plans specific. Ask an organized friend to help you make decisions about what to keep and what to toss. Set aside things to sell or give away—then give yourself a deadline to do it. If your deadline arrives and they're still sitting, toss them!

You may find it helpful to take pictures of any items you want to remember but don't want to keep. If actually letting go of the unwanted items proves too difficult, simply place them in storage boxes and set them aside in an out-of-the-way place like the garage. Dip into these boxes as opportunities to give things away arise. On the outside of each box, write a date on which you'll discard what's left.

It's hard to dispose of those things with which we have a love/hate relationship. Our ambivalence keeps us from making firm decisions about what to do with them. But when you finally do what your heart tells you is right, you'll experience a sense of freedom and power.

Start by moving out the things you can part with most easily. As you gain confidence, you'll find the job becomes easier and the pleasure you feel becomes even greater.

Day 11

Always Have a Backup in the Wings

Even the most capable person has times in life when best-laid plans fall through. A natural disaster hits. You become sick or tired (or maybe just sick and tired). Somebody else needs you full-time. You need to work overtime or do a big project. Things get lost. There are conflicts in schedules. Face it. These things happen to everybody.

Save yourself the frustration of trying to solve a problem when you are in the middle of it. You can avoid problems altogether by simply having a backup plan waiting in the wings. Like a Boy Scout, be prepared for the unexpected, so that when it comes—and it will!—you can seamlessly switch over to your backup plan.

Must-Have Backups

To ease the strain when plan A fails, consider setting up for yourself these must-have backups:

- *Old-fashioned "corded" telephone.* Sure, your cell phone and cordless phones are great—when you can find them and the batteries are charged and the signal is strong. But what about when you've misplaced the handset, or the batteries have run out when the power is off, or the cell-phone towers are out of service? An old-fashioned "corded" phone can save the day! It won't get lost and will still work when the electricity goes off.

- *A battery-backup power strip.* Like any other power strip, this device allows you to plug in multiple electronics, like your answering machine, computer, clock, and the like, all in one spot. But on a battery-backup model, when the electricity flickers off, the battery kicks in and keeps the electronics from turning off. So you won't lose your messages or have your computer crash. Your clock will not have to be reset, and your alarm won't fail to awaken you.

- *Computer files backed up.* "For all the sad words of tongue and pen, the saddest are these: 'It might have been,'" wrote John Greenleaf Whittier. And in no instance are these words more heartfelt than just after a computer crashes, taking your data with it, and you realize how long it's been since you made a backup copy of your work. At the be-

Lack of planning on your part does not necessarily constitute an emergency on my part.

ginning of each month, or preferably much more often, use whatever backup system you have devised, so you can avoid those dreary four words.

• *Fill-ins for you.* It's wise to keep your eyes open for personal and household help that can be your backup should you ever need it. Make a personal backup list that includes a handyman, house cleaner, lawn service, and the like. Watch for a high-school student who may be willing to help with chores around the house on a regular basis. Should you need help in the future, you'll already know whom to call.

Alert! Warning! Having a backup doesn't mean you keep on hand eight staplers, ten glue sticks, or an abundance of any other item, just because you can seldom find what you need when you need it. That is an entirely different problem and is solved by having a sane and usable storage system. Remember, order is maintained by rigidly following the queen of all habits: When you get it out, put it back! Now, not later. ASAP!

More Must-Have Backups

You'll save time and avoid frustration if you simply keep the following backups handy:

• *Nonelectric can opener.*
• *Disposable plates, cups, and utensils.*
• *A spare car key* hidden up under the chassis in a magnetic key container.

- *A spare house key* hidden outside where only you can find it. (No, not above the door!)

> **If you've made up your mind that you can do something, you're absolutely right.**

- *Your list of often used phone numbers* tucked in your purse for quick-and-easy reference.
- *An extra phone book* in the car for last-minute changes in schedule.
- *A standard plan for where lost children should meet you* if you should get separated. For example, older children meet at a central place, like the entrance; small children go to any adult behind a counter or in a uniform.
- *A photocopy of all the credit cards and important info* in your wallet, in case it's lost or stolen. Keep the copy at home.
- *A flashlight in a central location.*
- *A battery-powered, plugged-in emergency light* that automatically turns on when the electricity goes off. It doesn't illuminate the whole room, but it does give enough immediate light to help you find your way around.

Day 12

Simplify Your Solutions

If a simple solution can meet your needs, by all means, embrace it! Think KISS—keep it super simple. You'll make moving toward a more organized life easy if you KISS your way to order. Here are some ideas:

- *Do less laundry.* Pass out one towel per person a week. Change bedsheets every two weeks or more. Wear clothes more than once, when you can. (Slacks, skirts, and lightly worn tops often can be worn several times between washings.) Redirect children who want to change clothes (and towels) more than is needed.
- *Wear glasses that darken automatically in the sun.* My path was strewn with lost sunglasses before I changed over to a prescription pair that turn dark in sunlight and become clear again in the shade.
- *Cover your bed with a comforter or thick quilt.* A fluffy topper hides a multitude of wrinkles underneath. Perfec-

tionists, especially, spend too much time trying unnecessarily to straighten the sheets and blankets. The main question is whether it "passes" as a made bed. In bed making, a C grade is good enough.

Think KISS—keep it super simple.

- *Cook with nonstick cookware, and replace it when it starts to stick!* It cleans so easily. Sometimes all you have to do is swipe it with a little soap and water and put it back. It's far easier than putting it in and taking it out of the dishwasher.

- *Avoid complicating your life with "innovations" that don't work for you.* For instance, I tried the rechargeable-battery approach. It promised all good things. I approved of the savings and the ecological benefits. The only problem was that I never was able to use it. Remembering which batteries needed charging and which didn't, and where each group was kept, was just too complicated for me. Undoubtedly many people do it easily and can't understand what my problem is. I don't fully understand it either. The only thing I know is that for me buying already charged batteries is the best way (no, the only way) to go.

Sometimes the simple solution means giving up a complicated organizational trick. I confess that in my pursuit of order I tried keeping my spices alphabetized. I quickly found it more trouble than it was worth. There were numerous occasions when I have overorganized, only to abandon my system for something more effective and easier.

> There is no greatness where there is not simplicity.
>
> Leo Tolstoy,
> author of *War and Peace*

You'll simplify—and free up loads of space—if you miniaturize whenever possible. How? To get started, consider downsizing your

- *Christmas tree and ornament stash.* One of the smartest moves I ever made was to buy a two-foot artificial Christmas tree with lights already evenly distributed on the branches. Each year I pull it out of its compact box, fluff the branches, and it's ready for decorating. It needs fewer and smaller ornaments, so they take up less storage space, and I spend far less time trimming the tree. Placed on a pedestal table with gifts rising up from the floor, it makes a very fine Christmas presentation indeed, if I do say so myself.

The Miniaturizing Concept

Unless you have a very large house with broad expanses to be filled, whenever you can find a smaller appliance, tool, or anything that takes up limited space, select the smallest one adequate for the job. For most of us, finding enough storage space is serious business. Let a consistent and careful commitment to the concept of miniaturizing come to the rescue!

- *Bakeware.* My muffin tin makes only six muffins. That's plenty for Ivan and me. Previously I used half of a bulky, twelve-muffin tin that took up too much precious space in my cramped kitchen. Eventually I woke up to the fact that there were muffin tins with only six cups. An unexpected advantage is that the smaller tin fits nicely into my economical toaster oven.

> **Beauty of style**
> **And harmony**
> **And grace**
> **And good rhythm**
> **Depend on**
> **Simplicity.**
>
> Plato, Athenian
> philosopher (427–347 BC)

- *Appliances.* Speaking of toaster ovens, we need a new one. Ivan wants one big enough to roast a turkey, even though our counter is small, and I haven't roasted a turkey or anything like it in years. But I am holding out for (you guessed it) one just large enough for toast and muffins.

Coming Clean about Laundry

Think you're doing a lot of laundry and cluttering up your laundry room with too much stuff? You're probably right. Consider these facts from the Soap and Detergent Association:

- Women do 88 percent of the laundry.
- More than six thousand garments are machine washed each year in the typical home.
- The average consumer has eight laundry products in the laundry room—three types of detergent; one container of bleach; an oxygen-powered, color-safe bleach; two fabric softeners (a liquid and dryer sheets); and a stain remover.

Day 13

Wrestle That Email to the Ground

You step away for five minutes from your computer, where you've been striving to answer your email. When you return, you have eleven more messages stacked up in your inbox.

Email has the potential of being your biggest time-saver and friend.

Email is often a major source of frustration and wasted time.

Why the paradox? While email can make life easier by bringing you valuable information quickly, most of the time there's just too much of it! And so much of it is unnecessary!

Like a runaway steer, "that thar thing" has got to be controlled. So let's jump on the problem right out of the chute and wrestle it to the ground. Here are some of the ways you can take control:

- *Corral the junk before it gets to your screen!* If you're not using a good antispam software, statistics suggest that most of the email you receive is the electronic equivalent of junk mail. Your local office supply or electronics store should have a vast selection of software that can easily help you eliminate spam from hitting your inbox. Tip: Don't respond to spammers' messages, even to ask them to remove your name from their lists. That just spurs them to continue spamming you, because they know you're actually looking at the email.

  While email can make life easier by bringing you valuable information quickly, most of the time there's just too much of it!

- *Ask friends and family to stop forwarding messages.* It's nice that they want to pass along "cute" or "important" messages. And a lot of the information they send is good, I'm sure. But it's not good for you to have to deal with all of it. So just get up the nerve to send out a polite request to people in your address book. They'll get over it. And you'll be amazed at the time you save when you no longer feel compelled to open and read all of those messages.

- *Delete with enthusiasm.* Spammers are masterful at thinking of ways to make you think they are writing an important personal message to you. But if you don't know who sent a message or can't decipher what the subject line is about, press "delete" in a heartbeat. Whole groups can be deleted with one swipe, if you learn how to do that trick on your computer.

- *Take care of easy responses first.* Go to the email that can be dealt with quickly. If you can respond in just one or two lines, with thirty seconds of typing, do it! Get it off your radar. Get it off your screen. Get it off your plate. Then move on.

- *Write less!* You don't need to make each email your finest example of information sharing, wisdom, and prose. Just keep the conversation moving, writing quick responses. Stop composing the next great novel and burst out of the chute, or that steer will get away from you. If you've been waiting to respond to certain messages until you have enough time to do it properly, grab that bull by the horns, type an adequate response (not the perfect one you'd imagined), and move on—guilt free! By writing shorter messages, you'll save time for those who receive them too. A former agent of mine often responded to information I sent with a one word message—Noted. Now *that* is a quick response.

- *Don't catch the same steer ten times in a row!* You're bound to receive emails that could all be answered with the same

Email Clutter

Email is a kind of modern clutter prevalent both on home and business computers. A typical business user spends over two hours handling email. In businesses, 53 percent of users check their emails at least six times a day and 4 percent check it constantly all day.

response—questions such as, "So how are all of you? Tell me what's been going on!" Don't type the same lengthy responses over and over. Imagine the

time you'd save if you kept an up-to-date response for frequently asked questions, ready and just waiting to be sent out. Then you can use it whenever you need to, without having to rewrite the same information over and over again. Just write a good, generic, informative response—a kind of template—and save it in a place where you'll remember to use it. When you need to answer that kind of question again, simply pop open the template you've created, copy the bulk of the message, paste it into the email you're composing, and top it with an appropriate introduction. That will save you from retyping the same information over and over. Whew!

- *Save important messages to specific folders.* If you must save them, at least free up your inbox as a place that's just current information that needs to be handled.

- *Read what came in last, first.* It can save you oodles of time. Here's an example: I recently received a request to send a picture for media purposes. Later in the day, I received a message canceling the request, as the sender had found one. Because I'd started from the bottom of my inbox (where my most recent email waits to be read), I got to the cancellation before the request. That saved me the trouble of having to think of how I was going to solve the problem. Just figure out where your newest email waits for you, and always start working your way through it—newest to oldest.

> If you can't move the mountain, move a few stones.
>
> If there is a better solution . . . find it!
>
> Thomas Edison

• *Turn off the "auto-check" feature.* This is the one that checks your email and downloads new mail regularly, as often as you've commanded. Downloading frequently is important for some people who use email in business and have to know as soon as new messages come in. But for some of us, the notification that new email is waiting is too tempting to ignore, even if we don't *need* to check it right away. Computer experts who advise on boosting productivity tell us that if we don't have to have notification every time a new email is received, turn off the features that download it automatically and notify us instantly. Choose instead to download and check email when it suits *our* schedule.

Email will keep coming out of the chute. And that's good—much of it can make our lives easier. Manage it wisely, and you'll turn your computer-time rodeo back into a joyride.

At last count, studies suggest 30 to 62 percent of all email is spam. And though we can easily delete unwanted messages, the trouble is, we can't delete the cost. Experts at the Coalition Against Unsolicited Commercial Email (CAUCE) point out that spam costs businesses and consumers an estimated eight billion dollars a year. That's because all that spam costs Internet Service Providers, who have to buy more bandwidth to handle it all. So their fees go up. And spam overload often causes computer crashes, the CAUCE experts say, resulting in lost business opportunities, time on the job, even valuable information that must be re-created. How much worse could it get? If only 1 percent of the 24 million small businesses in

America send you only one piece of spam each year, you'll hit the delete key about 657 times, CAUCE experts say. Try clicking your mouse 657 times as quickly as you can. That shows how much time is wasted by spam, even when we delete it without reading it.

Day 14

Make Bold Judgment Calls

Sometimes the only thing that keeps us from making needed changes is one bold decision. What bold decision would make a positive change in your life? You might gain freedom if you'd

- *Drop out of a group or club.* Sure, you love the people there and they'd miss you, but is the commitment still good for you? Or could you gain needed peace by dropping out, at least for a while?
- *Give up leadership positions.* Can't bring yourself to drop out completely? Then just leave behind time-consuming leadership roles. Give somebody else a chance to do the job. You can take it up later if you want to.
- *Schedule one less sport or activity for your children.* Spend your extra time in a stay-at-home family activity, such as a weekly game night or reading-aloud-together time—anything less stressful than running around.

- *Give up addressing Christmas cards by hand.* Instead, create a mailing list that will allow you to print sheets of mailing labels or print the addresses directly onto the envelopes.

I did that for the first time this year, and I won't go back to the handwritten approach again.

- *Stop sending Christmas cards.* Okay, I know this is controversial. But if you're just too swamped at Christmastime, I think it's perfectly acceptable to send greetings at Thanksgiving, Easter, Valentine's Day, or some other holiday instead. The bonus: your friends and loved ones will have more time to focus on your card at one of these less busy times of the year.

- *Toss all mail with a bulk postmark—unopened!* We have to give up the curiosity that nudges us to spend valuable

What a Waste!

About 44 percent of all junk mail is thrown in the trash, unopened and unread. About 40 percent of the solids in our landfills are made of paper and paperboard. That's expected to climb to 48 percent by 2010.

time on the interests of somebody else (in this case, the company that sent the mail). I have a friend who says, We are not bulky people, so we don't need bulk mail.

- *Keep only one-quarter of your knickknack collection on display.* Knickknacks are dust collectors. Pack away three-quarters to be rotated back out on display later,

Stop Junk Mail

To remove your name from national commercial and nonprofit organizations' lists, write to the Direct Marketing Association (DMA), an organization representing more than three thousand direct-mail firms, service organizations, retailers, publishers, and catalog companies. Your name will stay on a no-junk-mail list for five years.

Just send your name (all the variations you use) and mailing address, with a request to remove your name from all mailing lists, to:

Mail Preference Service
Direct Marketing Association
P.O. Box 643
Carmel, NY 10512

Mail Preference Service
Direct Marketing Association of Canada
1 Concord Gate, Suite 607
Don Mills, ON M3C 3N6

Go to www.dmaconsumers.org/cgi/offmailinglist to register online ($5 charge).

maybe as the seasons change. Using this system, you'll appreciate them all the more. And you'll be less of a slave to dusting them.

- *Use the potluck system when entertaining.* You make a main dish and dessert. Let the guests fill in with breads, salad, vegetables, appetizers, and whatever else you think you need. This cuts down markedly on preparation and on cleanup afterward. For those who think proper etiquette requires a hostess to do it all, this will definitely be a bold decision.

- *Use paper plates when you need quick cleanup.* To avoid waste, use the smallest-size plates you need for each meal.

- *Give away unwanted, outgrown, or downright unpleasant items.* Many of these were probably gifts. For the sake of others' feelings, you may want to keep or even use them for a short period. But you did not make a lifelong contract to provide shelter for these things in your home. Bid them a fond adieu and let them bless others.

Save Time, Money, and Trees

Another great reason to drop your newspaper subscription, if you're not really reading it daily, is that it's good for the planet. Consider this: it takes 75,000 trees each week to produce the Sunday edition of the *New York Times*.

• *Cancel the newspaper and magazine subscriptions.* I believe strongly in a thriving press. However, we need to think carefully about how we are going to manage the flow of printed information into our homes. Try this: If you see something on the newsstand you'd like to read, buy it. But don't allow great gobs of paper to impose on you on a regular delivery basis. Canceling daily newspaper delivery brought me great relief when I began to seek order and simplicity for my life.

It may feel strange, at first, to make bold changes. Force yourself to do it anyway. The peace you'll gain will be worth it beyond measure.

Day 15

Save Time and Frustration!

Fatigue and time pressure, Mark Twain once astutely observed, have done more damage to families than anything else. It's "the almost universal condition of fatigue and time pressure," he noted, "which leaves every member of the family exhausted and harried. Many of them have nothing left to invest in their marriages or in the nurturing of children."

Wow, what a downer! But Mr. Twain tells it like it is.

Still, there is hope for change. Though we have different pressures than people experienced in his era, we can still make choices that help us manage our time wisely and find ways that are best for our loved ones.

Making the Effort Now

Often we can gain relief from the frustration of wasted time only when we take the time now to put a method in place that will save time later. Here are some ideas:

> We can make choices that help us manage our time wisely and find ways that are best for our loved ones.

Set up your phone to use automatic dialing. This is one of the best time-savers available. Invest fifteen minutes in learning how to program the phone, then enter the numbers you call regularly. You'll be amazed by the time you'll save in the future as you eliminate the need to search for those numbers.

Delete junk faxes. If you have a fax machine, you probably receive lots of faxed messages you don't want. You can easily eliminate junk faxes or ads. (Can you believe companies have the nerve to use your paper and ink to send you their advertisement, in your home, without your permission? I don't want to refinance my house, invest in penny stocks, buy insurance, or do any of the other things those faxers are pushing, and I surely don't want to pay for their unwanted sales pitch! Thanks for letting me vent. I feel better already.) To eliminate junk faxes, scan the fine print for instructions on how to call to be removed from the company's marketing list. This call is usually an automated, toll-free number, and you can complete the process in a jiffy. I have done this many times, and it definitely stops unwanted faxes. As time goes by, however, new faxers, like weeds, will drift in and need to be eliminated as well.

Add yourself to the do-not-call list. You'll save lots of time by heading off calls from telemarketers. To make it illegal for them to call you, log on to www.donotcall.gov or call 888-382-1222. If you register over the telephone, you must call from the phone you're registering. The registration lasts for five years. This won't stop calls from groups like political organizations, survey companies, charities, or companies with which you already do business. When they call, if you'd prefer they didn't call again, ask to be removed from their

> Before the reality comes the dream. We create our tomorrow by what we dream today.

calling list. If they call again, they could face an eleven-thousand-dollar fine.

Meet with Mrs. Crock-Pot regularly. Take five minutes to plop meat and vegetables into the Crock-Pot in the morning, and by evening you'll have a mouthwatering, time-saving, fragrant meal!

Jot down phone numbers as you dial them. Keep a paper beside the phone, maybe taped to the wall. When you call a number, note it if it's not already stored in your phone's automatic-dialing feature. Why? We often expect to dial a number just once, but often we end up needing to redial. Having the number nearby will keep you from having to go searching for it again.

Put an end to "quick" fixes. If you find yourself "fixing" something repeatedly, take time to fix it permanently instead. For years, every time I wanted to create a new document on my computer, I had to take the time to change the default font setting to the size and style I wanted to use. Finally I took the time (about one minute) to figure out how to permanently set it to automatically use my preferences. Whew! What a relief.

Look down the road for trouble. For instance, I bought a new front-porch swing, and there was more than a little assembly required. The job entailed fitting slats into a metal frame. Looking back, I see it would have been so smart of me (and not too hard) to have taken the time and energy to weatherproof those pieces before attaching them

Ideas become real at the point of action.

permanently to the frame. But did I do that? No-o-o-o. In my enthusiasm and, I might also admit, because of a bit of laziness, I put that thing together and hung it proudly. You can guess the rest of the story. Time passed. Now it is weather-beaten, and I will have to go through the time and expense of redoing it or buying another swing. I could have saved myself a lot of aggravation—and time and money—if I'd just taken time to do the job right in the first place.

Snatch the "best" times. Do you habitually schedule wisely? There are good times to accomplish certain tasks efficiently, and there are decidedly not-so-good times. For example, shop when stores are less jammed, avoiding the weekends when students and working people are most likely to be scurrying along the aisles with you. If you live in a big city, it's wise to schedule appointments or errands when it's not rush hour.

Scheduling Strategies That Save Time

Consider the time you waste whenever you're forced to stand in a long line or watch the minute hand sweep along the clock while you sit in a waiting area. Now, imagine how much more free your schedule would feel, if you could reclaim those lost, unproductive minutes. How would you spend that "found" time? Relaxing with loved ones? Immersing yourself in a hobby you love? Taking a few moments just to do nothing, with no pressures and no rush? Ahhhhh!

You can prevent your time from being unnecessarily wasted and reclaim those minutes. How? Simply employ these wise scheduling strategies with

Doctors and dentists. Request the earliest appointment of the day, before the office's schedule for the day is out of whack. The first

appointment after lunch is a good bet for being on time too, but the doctor may not be as refreshed as in the morning. After school, children mob doctors' and dentists' offices. So if you'd like a short, peaceful wait, that's something to consider too. Tip: If your doctor is a surgeon, request an appointment on a nonsurgery day.

Merchandise returns. Aim to be at the store when it opens. That's when it's more likely to be fully staffed with more-experienced employees—those trained to open the business. If you can't make it that early, at least try to avoid lunch-hour and after-work crowds.

Post office errands. Surprise—don't go to the post office as soon as it opens. Instead, plan to arrive about a half hour later. That way you'll miss the onslaught of early birds who stand in line, waiting for the doors to open. Save even more time by eliminating post office trips altogether. You can order stamps, calculate postage, track packages, and find zip codes online at www.usps.gov.

Hair salons. Again, ask for the coveted first appointment of your stylist's workday. That way you won't be left waiting through unexpected delays and, as with your doctor, you'll get your stylist's attention when he or she is most energetic.

Day 16

Attend to Little Things

King Solomon wrote that the little foxes spoil the vines (see Song of Songs 2:15). That wisdom certainly can be applied to the organization of your home. Neglecting one little thing after another insidiously ruins the order you are trying to achieve.

The opposite of Solomon's statement is also true. Doing a lot of small things consistently makes the "vine" of housekeeping flourish and bear a lot of really good fruit. By keeping up with these little things, you'll find an amazing transformation taking place. You will have more time. Your house will be more presentable. You will be able to find things more easily—all because of these small but powerful actions.

You'll begin to enjoy this result when you

- *Keep a list of items that need replacing.* Tally grocery needs on a whiteboard so whoever goes to the grocery store will get everything needed.

> We cannot direct the wind, but we can adjust the sails.

- *Return jewelry to its place as soon as you remove it.* It helps greatly to have enough designated drawers, hooks, or jewelry box space to hold your pieces.

- *Wipe water fixtures right after using them* so they always look good. The bonus: water deposits, soap, and mineral gunk won't build up and take a lot of your time and energy to get them off.
- *Stow empty hangers in a separate part of your closet* as soon as you remove the garments from them. Hang them in a designated spot on the bar or place them on a shelf within easy reach.
- *Serve dinner dishes on the kitchen counter* rather than family style to avoid spills and splatters. You'll save time wiping surface tops, washing tablecloths and place

List and Save!

About 55 percent of us admit we make a list— but don't stick to it. Simply shopping with a list can mean big savings at checkout.

mats, and cleaning up serving pieces.

- *Take an extra moment to clean up quickly when you're in a not-often-cleaned area* of your house. For instance, when you change the times on wall clocks twice a year, take a second to dust the top of the clock. When you retrieve something you dropped on a seldom-cleaned spot on the floor, like behind a heavy bed, make the effort to dust that area.

- *Put a new trash bag in the can* as soon as you take out the filled bag. Otherwise you or others will put trash in the unprotected trash can, or it will begin to back up on the kitchen counter. Ugh! to both of those. Hint: Store a few additional unused trash bags in the bottom of the can for easy access.

Kick Out the Bag Quickly!

When you pull the full garbage bag from the can, seal it and whisk it right outside without setting it down on the floor or (yuck!) a table or counter. Why? A garbage can is a breeding ground for bacteria. Given the right conditions, researchers say, a single germ can multiply 281 trillion times in 24 hours!

If you have a history of losing things, take heart. Scurrying to find misplaced objects seems to be built into life these days. In fact, studies show that the average American spends

> Not everything you face can be changed, but everything you change must first be faced.

approximately six minutes looking for car keys before going to work each day.

Imagine the time saved by always putting keys in the same place when you enter the house, like on a hook near the door or in a basket "holding area." It would add a half hour of free time to your week and a total of twenty-five free hours to your year!

One of the subtle secrets of organized people is that they consistently and somewhat automatically keep on top of such details.

Day 17

Circumvent Predictable Problems

Sometimes we ask for organizational trouble by not thinking ahead to avoid problems. We become so used to being insulted and frustrated by the conditions in the house that we begin to think of them as normal and unavoidable.

I used to suffer the same inconveniences over and over again because I never took the time to thoughtfully prepare to make things easier for myself. Finally I admitted that I would not let others do to me what I was doing to myself. This realization propelled me to make changes. Suddenly I could move more effortlessly through every day.

A few proactive steps can save time and work and keep us sailing smoothly in calm organizational waters. For example, you'll head off many predictable problems if you simply:

- *Buy a manageable bedcover.* You'll avoid having a soiled, messy look to your bed if you buy a duvet with an easy-on-easy-off cover. When your bed needs freshening, you'll be able to pop it in the washing machine effortlessly instead of wrestling with the whole comforter, which may be difficult to wash and dry at home. You'll have the additional advantage of being able to change the mood of your room just by changing the coverlet. Store several for seasonal change.

- *Write storage reminders.* If you split up like items in storage, place a reminder note with each stash reminding you where the other items are stored. For example, you may

Reflection on a Cleaning Schedule

I typed out a sheet of what I need to do each day, then a sheet for each room. On these I've put how often I do the jobs for each room, listing "Daily" first and going down to "Seasonal." I am figuring how often I really need to do each job and what cleaning/organizing is needed, making notes to help me remember.

have sheets in a hall or linen closet and extras in a box in the basement. Tape a note on the edge of the shelf under the sheets, saying, "More sheets in basement on second shelf." And if your stationery drawer won't hold all the envelopes you have, put a note at the bottom of the pile reminding you (or the family member who uses the last

Time-Out!

Have trouble keeping track of everyone's appointments, deadlines, and other commitments? You're not alone, but you can prevent scheduling snafus if you simply:

- *Post a family calendar in a spot where everyone can see it frequently.* **Use it to record everyone's appointments rather than trying to compare individual calendars. Keeping more than one calendar is like trying to ride two horses at once.**
- *Train everyone to record every commitment* **on that calendar. Some families use a different color pen for each family member. To keep pens from "walking away," attach them to the calendar with string or Velcro.**
- *Block out vacation days* **as soon as they're scheduled. This includes time off work, days the kids are out of school, or anything else that can affect your planning.**
- *Record final deadlines for projects,* **like filing income tax reports or completing a science project. If possible, record interim steps along the way. That will make those deadlines harder to ignore and will make it harder for them to sneak up on you.**

one) where the rest of the envelopes are located.

> You will never change your life until you change something you do daily. The secret of your success is found in your daily routine.
>
> John C. Maxwell, leadership guru

- *Sidestep dirty disasters.* Place soil-catching mats and rugs both outside and inside, so that by the time someone has entered your house, he or she has taken several dirt-shedding steps on floor coverings that catch soil and guard your house from unnecessary dirt. When you pare and clean vegetables, put down a paper towel to catch the parts you discard. When you crop snapshots, sort mail, or anything else that generates wastepaper, drag a trash can over and drop the paper directly into it.

- *Buy bigger.* When you purchase storage containers for a specific purpose—say for a filing system or gift-wrapping supplies—select larger sizes than you need at this time. You'll probably find you need more space than you expect as you add a little more now and then. And "buy tall" when getting a new step stool for the house. You'll need two or three steps more often than you think. Be careful, though! Don't buy jumbo plastic containers if your only use will be to dump a multitude of unrelated junk into it. In this particular case, smaller is probably better.

- *Be efficient.* Plan proactively by doing things like doubling up on cooking, putting aside some to freeze for a later meal. You'll never be caught again with nothing for dinner.

- *Make and use a workable to-do list.* A long list of unrelated items is unwieldy. I divide a page into quarters, labeling the four parts *Do, Write, Call,* and *Buy.* I learned this from professional organizer Marsha Sims. Then I categorize my tasks, writing each item under the proper heading. Beside each item, I draw a small box, because a box sitting there calls for the action of filling it with a check as the job is completed. Simply crossing the item off the list or putting a lone check mark next to it doesn't have nearly the same power for me as filling an empty space. If I do part of the job but it needs more work, I divide the little box in half, check only the first half, and leave the second half to be filled when the job is totally finished.

- *Call for appointments well ahead of when you need them.* This way you will have a better chance of reserving a time that's convenient for you.

- *Schedule cleaning/organizing time.* It may help to set aside blocks of time or designate "zones" of the house to be done each day. Having a plan helps you stay caught up and helps you avoid the roller coaster of cleaning binges followed by steady decline into disorder. Post a master list stating your plan until it becomes automatic.

- *Set up your house so that cleaning becomes almost effortless.* For a step-by-step guide on making adjustments to your home, check out *Make Your House Do the Housework* and *No Time to Clean: How to Reduce and Prevent Cleaning the Professional Way* by cleaning guru Don Aslett.

- *Set up a meal routine.* Post a list of the week's menus, shopping needs, and mealtime chores for the family, including setup and cleaning afterward. Often the family scatters as soon as the meal is finished because no one has taken time to divide the labor—a serious waste of kid (and husband) power!

Day 18

Abandon Extremism

Wanting to do things perfectly, or at least very well, is good. Sometimes. When the desire for perfection becomes a requirement, that's extremism. And that can be a significant hindrance to getting and staying organized. Consider whether you need to abandon the following extremes.

Recycling

My husband and I recycle paper and glass because our city picks it up every week. We also compost our raw fruit and vegetable scraps. But I've learned that it's easy to overdo and try to recycle every stamp-sized scrap and every seed. This puts us constantly on the alert and causes us to make little piles of scraps to be handled later. In the end, it junks up the house and wastes time.

Trying to do a good job of recycling turns into extremism when you save every empty margarine dish for reuse and every pair of old stockings for pillow stuffing. Materials to be recycled pile up in the house, garage, basement, or back porch. This is a problem.

Sometimes friends and family challenge us when we're overdoing something. If yours do, listen to them and change. If you're not that lucky, remind yourself that your house should be a place of order and beauty, not a recycling bin. It is a matter of balance.

Regret Avoidance

Don't fall into the trap of being so fearful of regret that you never get rid of anything. Feeling some regret when you get rid of things is an expected, even desirable, part of getting organized. If you never regret getting rid of something, it's a sign you are being too easy on yourself. Avoiding any and all pain interferes with the simplicity of an orderly life.

If you give away or throw away (gasp) some item and start to berate yourself for doing it, say "Yahoo! I'm doing it right!" It's natural to sometimes feel you have made a mistake.

I remember when I discarded an iron skillet—the traditional tool, used by us Southerners, for making corn bread. It had been passed down from my mom. But I had not made corn bread for years, and cast iron is hard to maintain. I didn't want it or need it. Discarding it was a defining moment for me. And would you believe it—the very next day I got a nearly irresistible urge to

> When we are authentic, when we keep our spaces simple, simply beautiful living takes place.
>
> Alexandra Stoddard,
> interior designer

make corn bread! That's precisely the destructive game we play with ourselves to keep from getting rid of things we haven't used in years.

> **A man is rich in proportion to the number of things which he can afford to let alone.**
>
> Henry David Thoreau

My mom, a neat lady who did not struggle with discarding as much as some of us do, once tossed out a watchband from my grandfather's Rolex. Later a jeweler told her the band was valuable. She discarded my brother's BB gun, much to his dismay. But she never seemed to feel regret because she knew that if you don't keep things moving smoothly along on a regular basis, clutter and messes will ensue.

If you play it so safe that you never make a mistake, you are not going to make progress. So accept those thoughts and feelings of sadness as okay, even helpful, on your journey to making your home a better place for you and your family. Your decision making will mature as you progress, and you will eventually learn to make fewer and fewer mistakes.

Niceties

Everybody knows that china dishware is nicer than disposable plates, and cloth napkins are nicer than paper. Everybody knows a handwritten letter is nicer than a printed or (groan) emailed one. We know handwritten addresses on greeting cards are better than computer-generated ones. It's very clear that a well-cooked, homemade meal beats takeout or frozen food. Certainly there are occasions when it's important to go the "nice" way.

But don't get stuck in the rut of always defaulting to the "nice" way just because you've

> **Prepare your heart. Pursue your dream.**

always done it that way and have never considered another way. Try shifting to a more casual lifestyle. You just might find it works better for you.

Do You Overdo?

Those who tend to overdo often do it in many areas of life. The result is an unwieldy struggle. It becomes difficult to make decisions, to move ahead on projects, or even to locate things—everything seems to be on hold until the "perfect moment" arrives. You may find yourself holding on to extreme habits like:

- Keeping all receipts—even for the ice cream cone you just ate!
- Saving all schoolwork papers while telling yourself that the children are little for such a short time.
- Holding on to memorabilia and too many toys from the past in an effort to remember the wonderful times.
- Not deleting emails, telling yourself that you will look at them more carefully when you have time.
- Storing all pictures ever taken. As a result, the "keepers" are lost among the bad and just plain ugly.

Wherever you see extremism creeping into your life, take a chance and change. Be bold! Be brave! Be tough on yourself and break out of old ways that feel familiar. Remember, rigidly going to extremes can hinder your progress toward bringing more order to your home and creating a stress-free life.

Day  19

Become Your Own Good Mother

Orderliness brings comfort. When the sunlight filters into a clean, beautiful, and organized living room, I feel like a child with a good mother. Someone cares about my well-being and has provided for my needs. Except that now, as an adult, I have become my own good mother.

Perhaps the chief reason that order is so important is that it chases away fear—the fear of being out of control. When I can't manage even the basic daily affairs of my life, my needs are not met and I worry—worry that my finances are in trouble and I may not know it, worry that someone will drop in and I will be ashamed, worry that I will need a receipt or important paper and it will be gone.

> Today is a gift. That's why it is called the present. Open it carefully, use it wisely, and don't forget to say "Thank you."

> The chief reason that order is so important is that it chases away fear—the fear of being out of control.

The good news? We can whisk away those worries when we simply care for ourselves the way a mother would. If a mother figure were to come to your house today, what would she do for you? Would she clean and organize the kitchen, vacuum and dust the living room, go through the closet and discard old clothes, or reorganize the shed?

Warnings of an Organized Mom to Her Daughter

My Dear, whatever you do, don't ever:

- *Put stuff in an unlabeled box or pile "just for now."* That creates a black hole of junk, and you may never see those items again—certainly not when you need them.
- *Bring home things without knowing where they will go.* Think hard about where you are going to put things before you jump for those "good buys" or "cute" items.
- *Save things for undesignated people or events, "just in case."* It's not your responsibility to overclutter your house to take care of possible future needs of the world.
- *Put unneeded things in needed spaces.* Don't stuff an item in a space just because it fits, like I did when I put old newspapers under the kitchen sink, then had no room for cleaning products.
- *Put off organizing just because you don't feel like it.* Act like an adult and "do the hard thing anyway." You'll be so glad you did.

Be your own good mother. Go now and do what is needed for yourself. Or hire someone to do it. In one way or another take care of yourself.

> Messiness is a disease of self-neglect.

You'll be treating yourself as Mom would if you simply

- Buy ahead so you can eat nutritious and tasty meals
- Clean a long-neglected spot
- Organize an annoying area of clutter
- Maintain an adequate wardrobe
- Obtain nice dishes, glassware, and flatware
- Buy what you need to make organizing work

And when the household needs are met so your home supports your needs, follow Mom's advice and indulge in yourself a little. Take the time to

- Soak in a warm bubble bath
- Exercise or take a walk
- Enjoy doing something artistic
- Read a book
- Get a haircut and manicure
- Get a massage
- Go to a movie or play
- Visit more with friends
- Get more rest

Day 20

Creep Up on Tasks

If you find that you are avoiding a job you don't like (I'm GONNA do it! Today I've GOT to do it! Well, maybe tomorrow), you may need to abandon the frontal-attack method. It's not working for you.

Instead, slide slowly sideways into the job. Soften it up, so to speak. Time-management expert Alan Lakein, author of *How to Get Control of Your Time and Your Life*, calls this the Swiss Cheese Method. Punch small holes in the project until it is done rather than attack the whole task at once. Punching small holes in it helps overcome our resistance.

Why We Resist

Sometimes our resistance comes from not being mentally prepared. Perhaps, for example, you want to color your hair with a new product, but you are hesitant because of uncertainties about how to do it. Punch a few holes in the project. You need information. Mostly you need to take a step forward to begin. To prepare mentally

> **Punch small holes in the project until it is done rather than attack the whole task at once.**

- Buy the product.
- Open the box and read the instructions.
- Call the number listed on the box for advice about how to use the product.
- With this information, estimate the time and tools you'll need to finish the job, once you actually start it.
- Gather the tools.

Do these steps, and then you'll know you can complete the job competently, as soon as you have the time to do it.

Sometimes we're just not emotionally prepared to do a job. For instance, you may need to clean the oven. You know how but hate to do it. To prepare emotionally

- Look in the oven and scope out the dirty spots. Get a lay of the land, so to speak.
- Reread the directions on the cleaning product. Is there enough in the can? How long does it take? Do you need gloves and do you have them?
- Place the cleaning product near the oven. In the near future, when the wind blows right and you have had a good night's sleep, you may find yourself spraying into a dirty oven. Shortly thereafter, with less work than you had dreaded, you will find yourself looking into a sparkling oven.

> When we strive for effectiveness and let go of perfectionism, we can achieve excellence.
>
> Beverly Clover

You can use this method with all kinds of projects: making those phone calls you've been putting off, cleaning the rug, straightening a closet, and so on. By getting the information you need, you punch holes in the project, allowing yourself to prepare mentally or emotionally. And suddenly, the task doesn't seem so overwhelming anymore.

Warning: Be careful using this system, or you'll have "project tools" sitting all around the house waiting to be used. Do this with only one task at a time.

Why We Procrastinate

Psychologists and researchers have found procrastinators put off tasks because of one or more of the following:

Dread Not!

Shaking the dread that comes with procrastination can make you happier—and healthier—researchers say. It's no surprise that studies show procrastinators feel instantly less anxious and guilt ridden once they get on task. But now studies also suggest that putting an end to procrastination can improve your *physical* health too. College students who procrastinate have higher levels of drinking, smoking, insomnia, stomach problems, colds, and flu, says researcher Tim Pychyl, Ph.D., associate professor of psychology at Carleton University in Ottawa, Canada.

- *False beliefs.* "I work better under pressure" or "I'll
feel better about doing
that later." Research sug-
gests the truth is this: last-minute work is often low quality, and procrastinating produces much more negative
emotion than just jumping into a job before a dreaded
deadline.

Just do it!

Nike slogan

- *Fear of failure.* They'd rather be seen as lacking in effort
than in skills.

- *Insecurity.* Believing they must be perfect to please others, their forward motion freezes.

- *Impulsiveness.* Unable to prioritize appropriately, they're
often distracted away from necessary tasks to do the
unnecessary.

- *Rebellion.* Their refusal to do a job is an angry message
to someone else.

- *The pleasure of pressure.* Some enjoy the adrenaline rush
of finishing a job, just before it's too late.

- *Depression.* When blue, all options can seem equally difficult and pointless.

Day 21

Find Out Where You Stand—or Fall

You're halfway there! You've finished day twenty of a forty-day program! You've probably made a lot of progress in your quest to become better organized, less stressed, and more at peace with the condition of your home. But you may feel that you still have a pretty long way to go. And that's okay. It's a journey. The path you're on is the right one. You just need to stick to it. Push on! Push on!

Maybe you're wondering, like a child in the backseat of the car, *Are we there yet? How much longer till we arrive?*

To get a better idea of where you stand—or fall—take a few minutes to answer the questions below. Knowledge is power. With the clarity you gain, you'll be better equipped to get back on that path and continue toward your goal.

For each question, circle the response that feels right for you—not the answer you think I'd want to hear.

1. There are parts of my house I won't let nonfamily members see.
   a. strongly disagree b. disagree c. no opinion d. agree
   e. strongly agree

2. There are disorganized areas in my house that I've put off tackling for years.
   a. strongly disagree b. disagree c. no opinion d. agree
   e. strongly agree

3. I cringe about how the house looks when unexpected guests knock on the door.
   a. strongly disagree b. disagree c. no opinion d. agree
   e. strongly agree

4. I have a hard time keeping up with my belongings. They are often misplaced.
   a. strongly disagree b. disagree c. no opinion d. agree
   e. strongly agree

5. I don't have a routine. I do things as I have time.
   a. strongly disagree b. disagree c. no opinion d. agree
   e. strongly agree

6. I buy groceries as I need them, or as they appeal to me in the aisle.
   a. strongly disagree b. disagree c. no opinion d. agree
   e. strongly agree

7. When I try to organize things, my brain seems to get muddled.
   a. strongly disagree b. disagree c. no opinion d. agree
   e. strongly agree

8. Getting rid of things is very hard for me.
   a. strongly disagree b. disagree c. no opinion d. agree
   e. strongly agree

9. I have piles of paper sitting around waiting to be dealt with.
   a. strongly disagree b. disagree c. no opinion d. agree
   e. strongly agree

10. If I could, I'd like to move out of this house and start all over in another one.
    a. strongly disagree b. disagree c. no opinion d. agree
    e. strongly agree

Add up the points as follows: **a** answers, **1** point; **b** answers, **2** points; **c** answers, **3** points; **d** answers, **4** points; **e** answers, **5** points.

10–17 Wow! I'm impressed! Can you come over to my house and give me a hand? Come to think about it, if you are too rigid about keeping order, maybe you need to relax a little, instead.

18–25 You're on a good road and your house works pretty well for you. You have been doing a lot of things right. Keep on making plans and carrying out those plans. Concentrate on the statements that got the highest number and vow to get better in those areas. Upcoming chapters will help you a lot.

26–33 You're pretty average, and that's not bad. Use this test as a chance to improve and help you move your house forward in the specific areas you identified. Upcoming chapters will help you create order and beauty. Pump up your enthusiasm by visiting model homes, carefully designed to have a "lived-in" look that's immediately pleasing to the eye.

Be inspired! You can have a home like that too! Keep reading to find out how.

34–41 You have a lot of unresolved anxiety about the condition of your house. You need to take better care of yourself. Address your needs by putting the tips in this book into practice. Check out other books that give a comprehensive plan, like my books, *The Messies Manual* and *Smart Organizing*, or whatever else rings your organizing bell. Commit to a plan and follow it. Any plan consistently followed is better than no plan at all. Tweak your routine to meet your needs as you go along. Keep reading. Keep working. You're getting there!

42–50 You are living a hard life because things are not working for you organizationally. You deserve better. A better way of life is out there waiting for you. As well as keeping up with your reading of this book, it would be wise for you to

- Get outside help from a professional organizer or an organized friend. Google "professional organizer" for personal and online help suggestions.
- List the problem areas you identified in the test, in order of importance to you. Begin working on solutions to those problems right away. Check the contents page of this book and skip ahead, if you need to, or go back and reread chapters that apply most to your current concerns.
- Spend a few moments now in thought about this fact: you may need to make major changes in your circumstances and behavior. If you keep doing the same thing in the same way, you will keep getting the same unpleasant result.
- Investigate further why you are having so much difficulty. Read my book *Messie No More* for enlightenment about why some people struggle with getting organized and others don't. You may find that now you are aware, you will notice help all around you that you overlooked before.

Day **22**

Watch Those
Four-Letter Words

We should bring things into our houses only because we planned for them and because we need them. Sometimes, though, we act impulsively (and therefore contribute to our struggle to create an organized, beautiful home!) because of these alluring four-letter words: *free, sale, cute, good,* and *nice.*

- *Free.* If we don't need something but take it only because we don't have to pay for it, it just becomes clutter.
- *Sale.* No matter how good the buy, if that's the main reason we buy something, we've simply spent money on new clutter.

Life is one long obstacle course, and I am often the chief obstacle.

- *Cute*. Perhaps this is the most appealing of all because it tickles our emotions in a very feminine way. But if it's just cute and not useful, it's still clutter.

- *Good*. Yes, it's a four-letter word too. There are many things at a garage sale, for example, that are "good" for somebody or something—Mason canning jars, for example, or a lovely, child-size, velvet dress. But if I don't can, and if I don't know any little girls who wear that size, those "good" items aren't good for me. Bottom line: if they're not "good" for you, don't bring "good" things into the house.

> If you find yourself admiring something that you haven't already determined you need, walk away.

Steal the Power from Four-Letter Words

If you struggle to resist bringing home things that are free, on sale, cute, good, or nice, you're not alone. Trust me! But you can diminish the power these words have over you by practicing resistance to them. So go ahead. Shop! (Another four-letter word, by the way.) And when you see something you love, pick it up, admire it aloud, enjoy it. Then walk away. The more you do, the more you'll be able to resist these four-letter words—and their intoxicating allure—in the future.

• *Nice.* "Oh, that's nice" is not a good enough reason for bringing more stuff into an already overstuffed home.

Beware of these four-letter words. They'll tempt you and pull your home in a direction you don't want it to go.

If you find yourself admiring something that you haven't already determined you need, walk away. And if one of these four-letter words pops into your mind, run! Maybe it really is free, on sale, cute, good, or nice. But when you get it home, it will become another four-letter word—junk.

More Four-Letter Words to Avoid

- *eBay.* A world of possible clutter—and expense—at your fingertips.
- *Deal.* It stirs up the thrifty side of you. Walk away until it subsides.
- *Want.* Wants come and go. If you really desire an orderly house, ignore those frequent and fleeting wants that add little more than clutter to your home.
- *Need.* Just because you might use it sometime doesn't mean you need it enough to take it home.
- *Give.* Fight that kindly instinct to take things home just because you want to give them away later.
- *Love.* You love many things. Remember, you'd love a serene life more—one that's free of junk and clutter.

Day  23

Do It the Easy Way

As you move through life, try moving in a continuous sweep, smooth and purposeful, like a dancer on the dance floor. Actually, make it a continuous swoop.

One of the things that sets apart people who seem to be organized all the time, so organized that they seldom, if ever, have to "get this place cleaned up," is this habit. They "swoop" everything quickly back into order, before it gets a chance to become clutter.

Here's a simple example: When you break an egg, swoop the shell directly into the trash, without putting it down on the counter to be moved later. By doing so, you eliminate living with an eggshell on the counter and also save the step of wiping up egg goop! This is the one-step method.

Dancing the One-Step

Not everyone dances the one-step. Some do the two- (or more) step dance. Here's what I mean. I'll use the coffee

One of the things that sets apart people who seem to be organized is that they "swoop" everything quickly back into order, before it gets a chance to become clutter.

example again in more detail. When making a cup, some of us

- reach for the creamer
- pour it in the coffee
- set the creamer container on the counter
- reach for the sugar
- pour it in the coffee
- set the sugar container on the counter
- reach for a spoon
- stir
- set the spoon on the counter
- put away the creamer
- put away the sugar
- put the spoon in the sink
- wipe the counter
- put the spoon in the dishwasher

Whew! What a workout!

It's far easier and quicker to do the one-step, returning the sugar and creamer to their places immediately, in one graceful swoop, without ever setting them down.

I've found that if you put sugar and cream into the cup first, the act of pouring in the coffee stirs it all together, saving the steps of getting, using, and cleaning a spoon. Another step saved!

If you still want to use a spoon, try rinsing and drying it immediately and returning it to the drawer. You'll be amazed by the amount of time that simple one-step process can save. It eliminates the clutter cleanup! You'll never have to go back and "get this place picked up."

I don't know much about dancing, but when it comes to doing the one-step, will you have this dance with me?

> There are two kinds of pain in the world, the pain of discipline and the pain of regret. The pain of discipline weighs ounces. The pain of regret weighs tons.

More Ways to One-Step

One-stepping things right back where they belong saves time and effort and creates valuable peace of mind. But to put things away quickly, you need to designate a place for everything. After you do that, you'll find jobs are accomplished more easily and won't pile up when, instead of dragging your feet, you

- *Put tools back* in the toolbox or on their spot on the wall, instead of just laying them near the door of the garage or shed. Next time you need them, you'll know right where to look!
- *File papers* in their proper place, rather than piling them on top of the filing cabinet.
- *Shelve videos, DVDs, or compact discs,* instead of laying them on top of the player.
- *Unpack and return your suitcase to storage* when you come in from a trip, instead of wondering, until your next trip, if someone stole your clothes.

> The bitterness of living in a mess remains long after the sweetness of resting is forgotten.
>
> Sandra Felton,
> The Organizer Lady

- *Remove clothes from the washer* before they "sour." Forgive me for suggesting this might happen. I speak here from personal experience.
- *Remove dry clothes from the dryer*—ASAP! It will save you from having to iron so much. Notice *iron* is a four-letter word.
- *Handle all groceries quickly.* This not only helps clear clutter, it's the safe thing to do. You never know when a cold item may have been put in with the canned and boxed goods.
- *Take purchases from the bag,* and put them where they should go. Leaving items in bags is a serious sign that your organizational abilities are grinding to a gummy halt.
- *Wipe the stove* quickly after use. It cleans more easily before the grease and drippings get cold and harden.
- *Slip sandwich ingredients right back* into the refrigerator or cabinet, after you use them.
- *Carry things in from the car* as soon as you get home, rather than making an extra trip out to get them later.
- *Drop junk mail into the trash* (or recycle bin) before sitting down. Some people even put a receptacle for that purpose right by the door, so junk mail never gets any farther into the house.

Day 24

Avoid the Quagmire of Passivity

In today's world, where most women don't have servants in the home, choosing to do nothing, when work is required, causes significant problems. We could all wish for a time and place when the house was kept orderly and clean by full-time maids, supervised by the lady of the house (that's us!). But it would be a fruitless wish. For most people those days are long gone.

Today housekeeping is a do-it-yourself job. Keeping the house in order is like running on a steep treadmill that never pauses. As soon as the kitchen is tidied, another meal begins. It seems we walk out of a neat living room, only to return to a messy one a few hours later. Bedrooms drift ceaselessly toward disorder with unmade beds and misplaced brushes, clothes, and shoes. Living is a process of progressive deterioration. Or so it sometimes seems.

Some choose a passive way to meet this relentless challenge of keeping an orderly home. But passivity just won't cut it in a world of burgeoning possessions and activities. However, aggressively changing a few activities will make a tremendous difference in the condition of the house.

Whence Cometh This Problem?

The Bible tells us that "by much slothfulness the building decayeth; and through idleness of the hands the house droppeth through" (Eccles. 10:18 KJV). Adopting a passive approach, with its resulting messes, carries a sense of personal and spiritual failure.

For our purposes, though, let's look at the problem of passivity dispassionately, without moral or emotional overtones. There may be several reasons for taking a passive approach to chores that need to be done. They include:

- *Physical.* People with low-grade physical illnesses, such as low thyroid or anemia, find it hard to get the work done. Often these physical reasons are undetected. These people appear just not to care, but they do.

- *Emotional.* Depression saps energy from and interest in many activities, especially those that are repetitive and unstimulating. And some women who were pressured into work when they were very young may try to show their independence by refusing to work as adults.

- *Educational.* A child who lived in a messy home or who was never taught how to keep house is at a disadvantage. A child who tried but never did it well enough for the one teaching her learned early on that she is "incapable" of keeping house. As an adult, she may cease to try.

> God, give us the grace to accept with serenity the things that cannot be changed, courage to change the things which should be changed, and the wisdom to distinguish the one from the other.
>
> Reinhold Niebuhr, twentieth-century theologian

- *Cultural.* Some cultures put neatness at a high priority; others have a high tolerance for disorder. A person from an easygoing society where messiness is no big deal struggles in a neater society where she is considered indolent.

- *Circumstantial.* Some situations make working so difficult that it's hard to overcome the discouragement. It may be a house that's too small, too large, or poorly designed with too few closets. Perhaps someone died and left you a lot of belongings—and you can't bear to part with any of them. It may be the work you do—for instance, farmwork that brings in dirt or a teaching job that requires a lot of papers and supplies. You may be renovating or cleaning up after a flood, hurricane, or some other disaster that makes it all just too much.

- *Familial.* Yours may be an uncooperative family, creating many messes but failing to help with cleanup.

> Take charge of your life. You are the only one who can—or should.
>
> Sandra Felton, The Organizer Lady

The best way to change is to recognize and tackle the cause of your lackadaisical attitude.

•*Entertainment interests*. Very few people prefer emptying the dishwasher to reading an exciting book. It takes an atomic bomb to blast a child away from the television or electronic game to feed the dog. With the entertainment opportunities in today's world, it takes a lot of maturity and training to develop the kind of habits that we need for an orderly life.

• *Personal characteristics*. Some people are visually alert and see things out of place. Some just move faster than others. Some naturally have more energy. These characteristics can help a person overcome the temptation to let things slide. But a person who lacks these characteristics will find it harder to build up enthusiasm for work.

"Behave" Yourself to Success!

You choose your behavior. So you choose the consequences.

The condition of your house today is the result of your daily repeated choices. If it's a mess, it's because you've chosen for it to be that way. If your house isn't beginning to change and become the tidy home you desire, it's because you are not changing enough.

I've got good news for you. You *can* "behave" yourself to success. You don't have to wait to *feel* differently or *think* differently. All you need to do is act right and the house will *be* right. And the more you choose to do the right thing, the less it will be a choice in the future—and the more it will become just an automatic part of life.

- *Mental outlook.* People who stay on top of things organizationally say they would rather do the work than have it preying on their mind. They love to check items off their lists, mental or otherwise. It gives them a feeling of power or happiness. But those who don't keep on top of messes seem willing to bear the burden of fatigue or don't seem to be suffering enough to make change worthwhile.

- *Relationship manipulation.* Sometimes people act passively to annoy someone else by not working. No one can *make* the person clean up, so he or she has the final "weapon" to use in an ongoing conflict.

Those who have fallen into a passive lifestyle find it hard to turn the tide and change their behavior toward a more productive way of life. Although they may be convinced, from a logical standpoint, that it would be beneficial to themselves and their families for them to behave differently, when all things are considered, they choose not to make the necessary effort. It takes a great deal of mental energy and positive motivation to alter any habit, especially one as pervasive as this.

But the effort is truly worth it. I promise.

Find Solutions

The best way to change is to recognize and tackle the cause of your lackadaisical attitude. Start by listing the problems that contribute to this pattern of life, and your turnaround will begin.

For instance, if you suspect your health is the root of the problem, see a doctor, get a diagnosis, and begin treatment. If chronic depression is the cause, it's time to face it and seek help. Even natural characteristics, such as a slow way of moving or visual inaptitude (the problem of not really "seeing" the mess), can be overcome, once they are recognized.

Once you are enlightened about what's causing your problem, you can do what's necessary to move into a life of productive activity, making a giant leap toward an organized life!

Is passivity interfering with *your* success? Start thinking now about what you can do to begin moving toward an uplifting and energizing way of life. Today!

Day 25

Embrace Old Sayings

I don't know about you, but I tend to find clichés a bit simplistic—and maybe a tad annoying. On the other hand, old sayings wouldn't last from generation to generation if there weren't a lot of truth to be found in them. Actually Grandma knew a thing or two that could help us. Let's look at a few clichés that have survived for many years because they contain a lot of wisdom—wisdom that can help you get and stay organized.

A Stitch in Time

A stitch in time saves nine. Can't argue with that one. I personally don't do much stitching, but it's easy to get the picture that if your seam is coming undone, the earlier you sew it back up (or staple it, as a friend of mine did), the less it will continue to unravel.

In the house, the sooner you wipe up a spill on the floor, the less likely someone will walk through it and track it all over the house. The quicker you clear the counter of clutter, the less likely clutter will continue to collect. (Clutter is magnetic, you know, and will attract more clutter to itself.)

If you wipe a greasy stove while it is still warm, you will do less work than waiting until it cools and hardens into gunk.

A Place for Everything

A place for everything, and everything in its place. Though this is a good statement, it would be great if it contained just one more bit of information: the location of the best place for everything. The fact is, to be truly useful, storage spaces must fit the job they were designed to do. For example:

- *Keep oft-used items close—within arm's reach or at waist level.* Seldom used items may be stored higher or lower. And rarely used items should be in deep storage, like the garage, attic, or basement, sometimes known as archives.

- *Group like items together to make finding them and putting them away effortless.* For instance, all tools should be together, all hair products, all photos, all craft items, and so on. You get the picture.

- *Store items in just-right containers.* Avoid the temptation to use very large containers, unless you are storing a very large object, such as a heavy comforter. When you use a large container to store a multitude of smaller things, they'll fit, but they're not easily retrieved. Once in, they tend to get "lost" and be unused. Small items need to be grouped in smaller containers.

- *Label the outside of every container.* At the very least, identify the category, such as children's art supplies.

Plan purposefully.
Prepare prayerfully.
Proceed positively.
Pursue persistently.

You may find it's worth the extra effort to list more specifically what's inside, so when you go to the storage closet, you (or someone else) can more easily find what's needed. This is especially important for containers holding items we rarely use. Use pictures as labels if your children are young.

Don't Procrastinate

Don't put off till tomorrow what you can do today. Okay, the limitation of this saying is that it's impossible to do *everything* today. Just thinking about it wears us out! No doubt we're limited by time, energy, and sometimes interest. The question is, which of those many things that we *could* do, should we do?

Organized people make it a habit to avoid procrastination. Some admit staying on top of everything just to avoid the burden of knowing a task is hanging over their head.

Those who are less committed to doing things expeditiously carry the burden of knowing many, many jobs sit waiting to be done. That's not good for them or for the house.

That said, overdoing this old saying can paralyze us. So to apply it wisely, I suggest making a list of ten things that need doing today. Choose the top one, two, or three and commit to completing those tasks. Tomorrow—even today!—you'll be glad you did. And so will others living in your house.

When a task is once begun, never leave it till it's done. Be the task, both great or small, do it right or not at all. Applied wisely, this keeps us from leaving jobs half done, with tools cluttering up the house, waiting for us to get back on task.

Bulk Up Evening Tasks— Slim Down Morning Tasks

Want to make mornings less rushed? Try shifting these traditionally early-in-the-day tasks to your nighttime routine:

- *Bathe the night before.* It takes some getting used to, if you're in the habit of a morning shower. But it really frees many precious morning minutes.
- *Fix lunches ahead.* But don't wait till too late in the evening, when you're already exhausted.
- *Lay out clothes for the next day.* This is one of the time-savers you can transfer from the morning crunch time to the more leisurely evening time. Make decisions for yourself, and help other family members do the same. Nothing messes up a perfectly good day more than an unwelcome rush of adrenaline that comes when you can't find one shoe or the blouse you need to complete the outfit you're already wearing.
- *Make your top ten list.* Note the ten things you want to be sure to complete tomorrow, so you won't waste time the next day trying to figure out what you need to do and when you need to do it.

But if we take "right" to mean that every job must be done with excruciating perfection and in intricate detail, this pithy poem will lead us to work our little heads off unnecessarily. Not every job deserves supremely excellent treatment. This is housekeeping, after all, not brain surgery or atomic research.

> Our most valuable asset is time, and successful achievers spend this precious commodity more carefully than money.
>
> Zig Ziglar,
> motivational speaker

When we interpret "right" to mean that it's appropriate to give the tub only a quick-but-thorough wipe after bathing, or pick up a few things as we walk by and return them to their proper place, then this ditty will steer us to develop a habit that will, ultimately, save us time, effort, even cash.

Prefer a more modern take on this advice? Here you go: Just do it!

Day 26

Don't Overdo Hobbies

Disorganized people are generally wonderful people with many really admirable qualities. And it's precisely these good qualities that often trip us up and lead us into disorder.

The Good Qualities

We are *mentally active* and excited about life's many opportunities, so we tend to try out a lot of different activities.

Because we're *family-oriented*, we want to produce heirlooms and ways to spotlight the people we love and to preserve memories of them.

We are *effervescent,* and as a result, we tend to lack boundaries. We let our activities take over the house, instead of devising ways to keep them under control. We tend to spend more time than we should on them as well.

Being *perfectionists*, we tend to overdo on the buying of products to support our latest hobby. We reason that it's important to have just what we need.

These good qualities often trip us up and lead us into disorder.

We *love to share,* so we keep producing an abundance of items to distribute to others.

We *live in the moment,* so we often fail to take note of how our actions will affect us in the future. For example, we don't think about how bringing all these products into the house, often without adequate storage preparation, will create clutter and disharmony.

Because we are *interested in a variety of things*, we often have several things going at the same time. When we become overwhelmed by tackling too many projects at once, we push unfinished tasks aside. Sometimes, we don't finish them—ever.

We are *imaginative* and can see possible uses for many different items. So we hoard castoffs and unusual items, planning to use them creatively later.

We are *frugal* and often buy products and equipment just because we believe they are bargains.

Keeping Hobbies in Their Proper Place

Perhaps you relish scrapbooking or quilting. Both activities involve piecing items together and therefore encourage the gathering of many items. This opens the door to excessive tendencies. Our good creative juices can flow out of control, and we can find ourselves drowning in pictures, memorabilia, or fabric scraps.

Maybe you enjoy collecting, painting, knitting, decoupage, needlepoint, embroidery, cooking, or sewing. All have their own special supplies and equipment that need to be controlled and organized.

Here's an example of what happens when we let hobbies get out of control. Martha has seventeen scrapbooks—a cross between a journal and a photo album—for her four-year-old, thoroughly documenting ages two through four. Every movement of every day is recorded. Think of the time required!

"The unexamined life is not worth living," the great philosopher Socrates said. I'm sure he never had *this* in mind. He did not say, "The *unrecorded* life is not worth living."

Nice scrapbooks and photo albums have a place. But if overdone, recording activities can become the purpose of the event instead of enjoying the event itself. Sometimes we just need to let it go and savor the moment, without fretting about how we'll remember it. If you love to chronicle life this way, or if you spend lots of time creating other crafts that are meaningful to you, look at the suggestions below. You'll save time, effort, even money; you'll end up with a better result; and it will be more fun.

- *Enjoy enthusiasm—with focus.* What I mean is, don't get so enthused that you take—and keep—too many pictures, hoard quilting scraps, buy an abundance of materials and patterns just because you happen on a "good sale" or something that's "really, really cute." Some people have more paper, scraps, material, patterns, yarn, or other supplies than any two people could use in a lifetime. Every hobby offers the temptation to overdo, and some of us are more likely to give in to that temptation than others.
- *Create an appropriate area in which to work and store supplies.* You can't always put a work-in-progress away.

So beware of turning the dining room into a permanent craft area or the bedroom into a workroom. Sometimes, like the camel who takes over the tent once he gets his nose in the door, what you begin as a small, short-term project turns into a bigger project that will take far more time and effort than you'd planned. When you see that beginning to happen, think seriously about how you can move the work to an out-of-the-way spot, maybe a spare bedroom or the garage. Hint: When a project needs to be put away temporarily, you might try laying out your work on large pieces of cardboard, then stacking them in order on a closet shelf.

> Beware the barrenness of an overcrowded life.

- *Buy only as you see a need.* If you purchase only a short-term supply of materials, as you see the need developing, you will be more sure of what is necessary. The bonus is you'll be letting the store handle the storage. (Why do you think it is called a "store"?)

- *Decide on your needs—before you shop.* Make a list and stay focused on it. If you do, you won't waste money on impulse buying, and you won't have to deal with the overabundance of stuff in your home.

- *Find and use smart storage solutions for your equipment.* Often hobby store clerks can make suggestions. Not only will appropriate storage protect small children from scissors, needles, paper cutters, and other dangerous equipment, but having a place to store your things safely will protect your project from being destroyed by curious little fingers.

- *Schedule a little time each day to reach your goals.* If you have a project that really needs to be completed, imagine how quickly you could make progress and eventually complete it if you simply set aside as little as fifteen minutes a day to work on it. As in everything else, you can make significant strides over the long run by just being consistent and doing a little at a time.

- *Remember, this is supposed to be fun.* If you get too caught up, and it turns into work, you've gotten offtrack. When the fervor to do a good job overwhelms the fun and you find yourself worrying at night and your way of life during the day is cluttered and unpleasant because of your hobby, you need to back up and get some perspective.

Your creative abilities are one of your wonderful characteristics. Just keep an eye on how they are working for you, and make the necessary adjustments. In the area of hobbies, "Easy does it" should be your motto.

Day  27

Let Mr. Technology Help

Technology can be a wonderful time-saver. I highly recommend using it whenever possible to make your life easier. But before you rush out to buy every electronic gizmo you can find, remember, there's a learning curve for any new technology. Choose only those devices that save more time than they take to use them.

For instance, I've known some people who started out using an electronic address book only to abandon it, because the touted time-saver actually made the chore more difficult. Now they're using a good, ol' little black book again.

That said, let's consider whether Mr. Technology might be able to make your life easier. Consider the following:

- *Computers.* If you're comfortable using a computer, it can serve as a time-management reminder tool to help you keep your calendar, to-do list, and much more. I use mine to remind me of birthdays, even though I also have a list posted on the wall.

One of the best uses for me has been addressing Christmas cards quickly and easily. I also enjoy being able to print and include a letter that summarizes the year, bringing my friends up to date with what's been going on in my life. That allows me to spend my time jotting meaningful, short personal notes, rather than the tedious task of copying details and addresses by hand. Handwritten is nice, but not nice enough to spend a lot of time on it.

- *PDAs.* Personal Digital Assistants are often known by their brand names, like Palm Pilot and Blackberry. Sometimes they are called pocket PCs. These little technology genies are getting more and more sophisticated. Available with a range of features, they can become the equivalent of a handheld office, with a phone, computer, radio, camera, video player, recorder, and more—all in one! Technology is moving so fast that by the time you read this, PDAs may even be milking cows or mopping floors!

A man in an airport told me he can do all his work while he travels. Thanks to the features on his PDA, by the time he gets home, he has his work complete and out of the way. And his PDA allows him to be so efficient and plugged-in, so to speak, clients and associates aren't even aware he's not in his office.

An author friend carries her PDA with a plug-in keyboard in her backpack when she travels. She writes as she travels, then downloads her work into her computer when she gets home.

- *Cell phones.* These have become so common, they're now part of the fabric of the lives of many individuals and families. They help families keep up with plans they have in progress. Some include a calculator and calendar. Some now come with the ability to send written "text" messages, surf the Internet, send and receive email, and shoot and send photos. Some even have global-positioning capability.

- *Smart phones.* Home and cell phones are becoming smarter and smarter. For example, some can be prompted to add the last caller to your speed-dial list of numbers, and some new phones can automatically transfer that list from phone to phone using a movable chip. Learning—and using—all the shortcuts available on your phones can save you valuable time.

- *Hands-free telephone headsets.* Headsets allow you to use your phone without holding it to your ear, leaving your hands free to dust, take care of the children, empty the washer, whatever.

Fast Fax Facts

There are now more than one hundred million fax machines worldwide, and faxing accounts for 40 percent of total telephone expenses.

- *Call-screening devices.* You don't have to sprint for the phone every time it rings. Try screening callers with an answering machine or your phone's Caller I.D. feature, which displays the caller's name and number. Then you can pick up only the calls that relate to your interests and needs.

- *Fax machines or eFax services.* "Get a fax machine," a man once told me and said I would thank him a hundred times for the advice, if I followed it. I did get one, and he was right—it has been invaluable. Other people choose to use a computer faxing system, like the one that can be downloaded and used for free at www.eFax.com. If you do any business from home, I'm sharing this with you so you can thank me a hundred times too. By the way, thanks again, Pete.

- *Navigational systems for your car.* Though it can be pricey, this technology can simplify your life by guiding you smoothly to destinations without getting lost.

- *Digital music players.* Storing your music in an iPod or similar device allows you to carry up to, literally, ten thousand songs in a portable player that's smaller than a deck of cards. And because iPod and other players can be remotely played through any home or car stereo, they eliminate the need to cart around CDs you want to enjoy. If your computer system has enough memory, you can even store (and instantly organize) your entire collection on it.

- *Digital cameras.* Shooting digital photos simplifies your life by allowing you to know, right away, whether you got the shot you wanted. And the camera allows you to delete right away the shots you don't want to keep. There are no negatives to keep up with, and you don't have to go to a store to have them printed if you'd rather print them at home.

- *Scanners.* Using a scanner, you can store snapshots, documents, children's artwork, and much more on your computer, compact disc, or DVD, rather than fill filing cabinets with the hard copies. This will take up less room for sure, and it's useful in some situations. But consider that technology changes quickly. Will you still have hardware to access those pictures in

Can Your Phone Do This?

Using cell phones to take digital pictures is becoming so popular, 56 percent of people think camera phones will replace digital and film cameras in the next ten to twenty years. A poll of thirty-five hundred women in the U.K. who use camera phones revealed that:

- 20 percent take photos of themselves in new clothing to send to friends
- 18 percent take photos of clothes and shoes in shops
- 15 percent take photos of the sides and back of their hair
- 10 percent use the phone as a mirror to check their makeup
- 5 percent take photos of well-dressed people to copy their look
- 4 percent use their phone as a mirror in a restaurant to check their teeth

fifty years? Maybe not. Printed pictures, well-preserved in an acid-free environment, may have a better chance of being available for posterity. Warning: This technology also may seduce you into keeping more snapshots than you should, just because you can. Don't use it to avoid getting rid of poor-quality snapshots that you know in your heart should go.

- *Automatic toll-paying stickers.* If you use toll roads regularly and your state offers an automatic toll-payment device, invest a few minutes in getting that set up in your car. It will allow you to zip through toll plazas, without having to stop and fumble for change.

- *Online bill-paying programs.* If it's available through your bank, this service can organize your bill paying instantly. You'll spend a little time entering basic information. But after that, sending payments for bills becomes practically effortless—and you could easily save forty dollars or more on postage each year.

If you work with Mr. Technology on a regular basis, you know how powerful he really is. Even those of us who are technologically challenged will find we must make him part of our lives, like it or not. So get on very good terms with our friend Mr. Technology, and let him help you make life easier.

Day 28

Focus Intently on Laundry

Of all housekeeping tasks, two top the list of being difficult to manage when we are disorganized—handling paper and keeping up with laundry.

When it comes to laundry (I'll talk about paper later), it's not the washing and drying that are the problems. With today's modern machinery those tasks are easy. In fact, the ease with which laundry can be washed and dried actually precipitates many of the other problems. Because it's so easy to wash, we

- *Accumulate too many garments*—often because we want to avoid frequent washings. If we had fewer clothes, we'd certainly be more efficient in moving them through the pipeline. But having a lot of clothing ends up being counterproductive and makes a bigger problem because it allows us to go longer without doing the laundry. Pareto's Principle suggests that we usually wear 20 percent of our outfits most of the time. The other 80 percent just gum up the laundry process and crowd the closet.

• *Change linens too frequently.* For example, instead of being hung on the towel rack to dry, once-used towels often land on the floor or in the hamper.

• *Change outfits too often.* People in today's world change clothes far more often than in the past when washing was done by hand. A historic school documentary on hygiene suggests students change their underwear twice a week. (Yipes!) We certainly don't want to go *that* far to conserve clothing use, but even fastidious adults should be willing to wear some garments two or three times between washings. And kids may be able to stretch use by changing into "play clothes" when they come in and hanging up dress clothes for another wearing. Kids (even husbands) will often throw clothes and towels, sometimes perfectly clean ones, in the laundry just to keep from making the effort to hang them up. But you can train them—and yourself—to minimize laundry by maximizing wearing time.

And there are more savvy solutions. To cut down your laundry burden, make a point to

• *Sort it out.* Sorting is an annoying task that causes many of us to avoid laundry chores. When we sort clothes that have been in a large hamper, they end up in unsightly piles on the floor waiting their turn in the washing machine.

But there are easy solutions. One is to wash most of the clothes together in cold water. Some newer products clean even heavily soiled loads well using cold water.

If you don't sort, it's important to use a dye-absorbing product to keep lighter clothes from being ruined. These products are available at the grocery store. I use Dye Magnet, but there are several other brands as well.

Another way to end sorting woes is to presort colors as you take them off by tossing them into color-designated hampers—one for bleachable whites, one for light and bright colors, one for darks, and one for delicates. Training your family to toss their clothes into the right hampers could save an hour or more of sorting each week!

- *Be on hold till you fold*. Dread folding, especially when you're facing a mountain of clean clothes? You're not alone—this is, by far, the most common stumbling block to laundry success. But you can make life easier—and more pleasant—if you simply limit the number of loads

Self-Cleaning Clothes!

Scientists have discovered a way to keep dirt from adhering to fabric, while warding off body odor as well. Garments made with fabric treated with this new substance won't feel any different but can be cleaned with a simple rinse. Dirt—and the water too—will slip right off! The method they're developing was inspired by the perpetually clean, white lotus plant, found in the swamps of Asia. But don't throw out your washing machine yet. The new fabric probably won't be available until 2009.

you do. If that's not possible, vow not to wash a new load of clothes until the one before it is folded. The task will seem far less overwhelming that way.

- *Put clean clothes in their place.* Sometimes, we get the clothes washed, dried, and folded, then heave a sigh of relief that the job is done. Piles sit folded in the basket, on the living room floor, wherever. Items on hangers grace our décor. Say it isn't so at your house!

  Try changing your mind-set. Tell yourself the job is not done until the clean laundry is safely home in drawers or closets. Following that rule will save you from loads of unnecessary washing. Why? When clean clothes are put away quickly, they can't be carelessly mixed with dirty clothes in need of washing—a common occurrence in kids' rooms.

- *Stick to a system.* Find a pace that keeps things moving. Decide on a plan that moves you forward consistently. One working mom puts a load in every day as she heads for work. Her husband, who gets home from work before she does, puts them in the dryer when he gets home. Later that evening, they fold and put away together.

- *Recruit 'em young.* With training, your children should be able to do their own laundry by age eight. They'll get into the groove the first time a favorite outfit isn't clean and ready to go when they want to wear it.

- *Attack stains early.* There are two basic kinds of stains—protein and grease. Read the labels of stain treaters in your grocery store and buy one that can wipe out both kinds. Keep it close to the hampers where you toss just-worn clothes. If your stain-treating product doesn't forbid it, treat the stains as soon as you remove the clothes. Not only will this practice make the stains more likely to disappear on the first wash, it will save you from having to search for the stains later—if you even remember they're there.

- *Tame the inside-out monster.* Some clothes come out of the wash inside out because they were tossed into the hamper that way. You'll save time by teaching your family to help you by simply having them turn clothes right side out before tossing them into hampers. If they resist, hang clothes or fold them just as they come out of the wash. The person who wears them can turn them properly and will quickly learn to do so *before* washing. (Note: Some clothes wash best inside out.)

- *Bag delicates.* Tuck stockings and other gentle-care garments in an inexpensive, mesh laundry bag designed for that purpose, then toss them into the appropriate load. That way lace and other delicates will be protected from

One Person's Reflection on Training Kids and Reducing Wardrobes

I fold the clothes every evening (when the kids are asleep, and I'm watching the news), then in the morning, they put them all away. I also teach them to put them in their drawers in sets, so everything matches. I'm working on getting rid of a lot of clothes. The less they have, the easier it is.

Blanca

tearing and twisting. Remember to close bra hooks so they won't snag other items.

- *Get the skinny on towel control.* To cut down on too frequent towel washing, select thinner (and less expensive!) bath towels, especially if you live in a humid climate. The thinner they are, the faster they'll dry. Or use hand towels for drying after bathing because they wash more easily and dry faster.

  Sound strange? Not really—just smart. You may have seen competitive swimmers and divers in televised sporting events dry themselves using funky looking, small, thin towels. Why? They dry the body very quickly, wring out well, and wash and dry easily. Sold in sporting goods stores, these "swim towels" or "sports towels"—about nine to thirteen dollars—are not luxurious, but used in the home, they can take serious pressure off towel washing.

  Some people go to great lengths to avoid excess towel washing. One woman told me she uses a washcloth to dry herself after bathing. I'm not making this up. That certainly would cut down on stuffing the hamper. I tried it, but found I ran out of dry cloth before I ran out of wet body.

  Another woman told me that when she was a child, her family used one fresh towel every day. (I recommend one per week, per person.) She has no children but still wants to conserve towel use. So now she drips-dry, she told me. Perhaps she was kidding.

I think you'll find a more satisfactory result by putting the rest of these tips to use. The payoff will be a less cluttered home, cleaner clothes that last longer, and a big savings of time, energy and, in some cases, even cash!

Day  29

Free Yourself from the Burden of Options

One of the reasons we tend to keep so many things and plan so many activities is because, as I have heard people say, "we want to keep our options open." I've also heard this: "I have a hard time making decisions because I see so many possibilities." That's the danger of having too much—too many things, too many clothes, too many activities. We suffer when

- *We pack too much for a trip* because we want to make spur-of-the-moment decisions. We don't know how we will feel like dressing or how others will be dressed or what the weather will be. So we have to drag the heavy case, spend additional time to pack, and take more time to unpack.

- *We keep coupons for things we seldom or never buy* because we might decide later that we want an item. That creates clutter—and for many, guilt, because the stacks of

Do yourself a favor. Set boundaries in your thinking ahead of time, so you won't have to deal with so many choices.

unused and expired coupons suggest to them that they're not being thrifty enough.

- *We collect materials for hobbies and activities* that we will likely never use, but we store them away, just in case we get the urge. We spend money for things we don't use. Meanwhile, the paints and glue dry out, and the supplies clutter the house. By "keeping our options open," we waste money and create the discomfort that comes from disarray.

- *We have too many lipsticks and blushes.* We paw through our makeup drawer trying to find the good among what has become bad. We have colors that don't match our complexion, our clothes, or the current style. Who knows what has dried out or grown bacteria over time? But whether good or bad, we certainly have made sure that we have many choices!

- *We have clothes and shoes in our closets that we never wear,* but we want them in the closets so we can have—you guessed it—options.

Do yourself a favor. Set boundaries in your thinking ahead of time, so you won't have to deal with so many choices. Jettison superfluous stuff. Make your life more "lean and mean." It will be a relief.

At first, as you clear out your "options," the process will make you uncomfortable. But remember, you do not have to gather an abundance of items about you in an effort to be covered, "just in case." If you are doing this, you are carrying an unnecessary burden.

> There is no greatness where there is not simplicity.
>
> Leo Tolstoy,
> Russian author

So bite that decision-making bullet. It may help to say to yourself: This item is good, but it is not good for *me* at this time.

From time to time, you will undoubtedly be sorry you got rid of a particular item. That is part of the process and is to be expected. It's even desirable. It means you're doing it right. Take heart in that!

Always follow the Rule of Three: Don't buy a piece of clothing unless you have at least three other pieces to wear with it.

Simplify Your Wardrobe

"I have a lot of clothes, but I can never find anything to wear. Nothing matches!" How many times have you said it? If you're like most of us, you've said it or thought it often.

How does our wardrobe get so full of stuff we don't like and don't wear, leaving us lots of options but none we really like? Most of us fall into the trap of buying clothing only because it's "cute," on sale, or simply fits. But there's a better way—one that will help you get dressed easily for every occasion. Streamline your options!

Stock your closet with items in a few basic colors. Then you'll easily mix and match basic pieces. And you'll always feel pulled together. Black, beige, red, and navy are good choices for most basic pieces. Other colors become popular, then fade in popularity, and can make a once-fashionable outfit look dated.

I choose lots of black and burgundy pieces, adding white for accent pieces, and other colors, like lime green, as they're in style. Your color choices don't have to be the same as mine. But you get the idea.

Allow only a few colors through your closet door. If you strongly desire other colors from time to time, work them in

> **No amount of things can fill a hole in the heart.**

with accessories. Always follow the Rule of Three: Don't buy a piece of clothing unless you have at least three other pieces to wear with it.

The moral of the story is this: Don't cause yourself stress by having too many color choices and patterns in your wardrobe. Buy mostly things that go together—in many different ways.

Don't let renegade pieces invade your color-coordinated kingdom of clothes. Get a plan and work the plan, adding only useful pieces to your wardrobe.

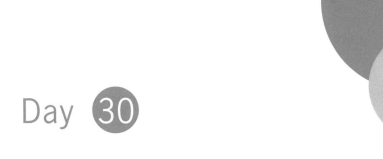

Day 30

Simplify Your Paperwork

Papers cause the number one problem in organizing because it's so easy to keep them and so hard to manage them. Papers are small and take up little room individually, so we lose sight of how much room they'll take up when they're piled on top of each other. And it's so easy for important papers to become mixed in with unimportant ones—and lost!

The chief problem with paper is there's so much of it. Rather than diminishing the amount of paper, the computer has increased it. Then, of course, there are school papers, newspapers and magazines, receipts, mail . . . well, you know better than I do what you have in your house, piled on the dining room table, desk, or bedside table. How should you handle all this paper? The following four basic steps of organizing are more crucial when dealing with paper than with anything else.

- *Simplify.* Keep only the papers you'll need later. If they can be easily replaced, throw them away.

147

- *Sort.* Group like papers, such as bills, receipts, bank statements.
- *Store.* Plan a paper pathway, so each has a definite home. Boldly label the spot, file, or container where each kind of paper will live. Avoid tossing any into the organizationally disastrous "miscellaneous" pile.
- *Systematize.* Develop a routine for handling the papers that enter your home. Set aside a place, time, and method for working with each one quickly and efficiently.

Let's talk about simplifying now. We'll deal with the other *S*s in the next two chapters.

Simplifying, when applied to paper, means guarding against excess. Don't let unnecessary papers into your house. Period.

Because we are curious people who love new ideas, we may be tempted to pick up a pamphlet, for example, on hydroponic gardening techniques in China, even if we never garden, don't plan to, and are not Chinese.

Paper Clutter

Paper is the biggest source of clutter. Even with computers, the volume of paper has more than doubled since 1995. Although we use only 20 percent of the paper we keep, 90 percent of information is on paper. U.S. businesses spend $25 billion a year filing and retrieving paper.

One woman told me she collected information simply so she could be sure to have interesting things to say in conversations. This is a society saturated by electronic, as well as printed, news. Trust me—it's highly unlikely you will ever be information hungry.

Fear of an IRS inquiry makes many of us keep too many papers. And if you're concerned that you're throwing out information you may need later, by all means, give a quick call to your accountant or tax preparer. But otherwise, as often as you can

- Avoid bringing home interesting-but-unnecessary papers.

Discard Papers Expeditiously

Though not all financial experts agree on how long you should hold on to "important" papers, this is a general guide. If you have a special reason for keeping them longer, these may not apply specifically to your case:

Tax returns and records—six years
Real estate records—as long as you own the property
Insurance policies—as long as they are in effect
Bank and investment statements—until tax time
Pay stubs—until tax time
Utility bills—until the next statement comes
Credit card bills—until the next statement comes

Copy, clip, and tape this list to your filing cabinet or wherever your records are kept.

- Toss junk mail in the trash or recycle bin as you sort the mail.
- Cancel magazine and newspaper subscriptions, get your refunds, and buy only the issues that really interest you on the newsstand.
- Toss unnecessary receipts before leaving the store. After all, you are not going to return the hamburger and fries you just bought and ate. Hint: If there's personal information on the receipt, marking through that part with a pen or tearing the receipt into small pieces is a good idea.
- Cancel catalogs.
- Stop the avalanche of "preapproved" credit card and insurance offers by calling 1-888-567-8688.

Follow these tips, and you will immediately reduce the anxiety that excess paper causes in your home.

Day 31

Sort and Store
Your Paperwork

Incoming papers can usually be sorted into four categories rather easily. And each category needs its own separate container. Those containers are:

- *Trash can.* The bigger it is, the more likely you are to use it. Have it handy, and fill it with joyful abandon.
- *Read-me file.* Here's where you put things you want to read at your leisure, such as letters from your college alumni association or your favorite ministry.
- *Act-on-it file.* The note from the dentist saying it is time for your annual checkup goes here, along with bills that need to be paid, and other documents that should be dealt with quickly.
- *Save-me file.* Some paper you'll need to keep handy temporarily, like the list of dates for your child's soccer

games. Other papers, like the latest car insurance policy, need to be put into long-term storage, as in a file box or filing cabinet.

Keeping Them All Straight

How do you sort all the papers? First, determine where you need to do it, then choose an organization tool to keep there, such as a set of inexpensive stacking trays or a file box that's open at the top, so things can be slipped in easily. Then commit to dealing with papers immediately, as they come into your home, slipping them right away into their proper spot.

For long-term storage, a four-drawer filing cabinet usually has plenty of space. My friend Marsha Sims, a professional organizer, divides the files of her clients into People, Places,

One Person's Reflection on Handling Mail and Bills

I used to have a very difficult time finding my bills. I finally got a very nice basket that sits on my computer and holds them all. Nothing else goes in there. When I get my mail, I open it in front of the shredder. Things I don't want are shredded immediately. Bills go in the basket immediately.

Leslie

Things, Money, and—for those who bring home tasks from the office—Work. File your papers this way, and you'll never wonder where to look for them when you need them again.

Sometimes, however, when you come in with mail in hand, you have to stop immediately to do something else—answer the telephone, feed the baby, give older children a snack, and so on. Soon the mail (wherever it has been put down) is forgotten. To prepare for these times when you can't jump right into your quick, four-category sorting, simply create a "holding area" for incoming papers. A basket, kept near the door you usually use, works well for this. You can place mail in it as soon as you enter. Just be sure to get back to it regularly. And if you usually enter through a side or back door, put a trash

> You will never change your life until you change something you do daily. The secret of your success is found in your daily routine.
>
> John C. Maxwell,
> leadership guru

Did You Know?

Studies suggest 23 percent of us pay bills late—and incur fees—because we lose them!

According to a recent study, the average U.S. executive wastes about one hour a day—for a total of six weeks each year—searching for documents lost in clutter.

can nearby for obvious junk mail. Just no trash cans in the living room, please.

Some items will need to be handled at a future time. For them, set up a "pending" area, maybe in a file or another small basket. Limit the height of it, though, so you'll be sure to attend to it before it becomes the Leaning Tower of Paper.

Day 32

Work Your
Paperwork System

Consistency! Consistency! Consistency! That's the key to making any organizational system work, especially when it comes to handling paper. Consistency is so important that the mere act of using a system, day in and day out, is far more important than having a good system. Whether your system is a brilliant idea or one that still needs some refining, the key to making it work is to work it consistently. There's just no substitute for that.

The worst thing you can do when handling paper is to drop a piece on a table and put off a decision of what to do with it. Misplaced perfectionism fuels a dangerous desire to do the best possible thing with that piece of paper, so you put it down until you decide how to handle it properly. That is a very imperfect decision, one that causes clutter, chaos, and unnecessary angst.

> Done is better than perfect.

You've taken the first steps in handling paperwork properly by learning to simplify. That keeps unnecessary paper from coming into the house. You've set up (I hope!) appropriate storage containers for each kind of paper. Now you must commit to following your plan each time you have a paper in hand—right away. If the containers for papers are clearly labeled, easily accessible, and simple to use, you can move forward easily.

Your filing cabinet is your best friend for long-term storage. Make an "Important Papers" section for mortgages, insurance policies, wills, and the like. Then place those papers alphabetically in that section. Make a master list of the section and

The Cost of Filing Too Much

It's important to make sure you don't let perfectionist tendencies lead you to file too many papers. Not only does this waste your time, space, and effort, it's pricey too.

Researchers studying the way we handle paperwork have determined that it costs a business about twenty-five thousand dollars (in employee time, materials, and so on) to fill a four-drawer filing cabinet, and more than twenty-one hundred dollars a year to maintain it!

Your time is valuable too, even though you're not paid for your around-the-house chores like filing. Protect your time by filing only what you really *must* keep.

put it in the front of the drawer or on the side of the cabinet so you can easily determine what's in there.

> **Genius is 99 percent perspiration and 1 percent inspiration.**
>
> Thomas Edison, inventor

Sometimes kindly insurance salesmen will give you a folder for your policies. If this happens, discard the pretty folder. It's not part of your system. Instead, quickly tuck the policy into the "Important Papers" section of the file under Insurance. If you consistently use the system like that, you'll always know where to look for your most important papers. Follow through, and you'll thank yourself for doing so for the rest of your life.

Day 33

· Zap Hidden Hindrances

Feel like you're sometimes stumbling when it comes to implementing your newfound organizational skills? Can't quite figure out what's tripping you up? Still feel like you just can't quite get everything under control? That's okay. Really!

Sometimes, in our pursuit of a saner and more organized lifestyle, we're the last to see what's snagging us and pulling us back. I remember my amazement when I conducted a survey on how many drawers people had in their living space. To my amazement they would start mentally counting and saying as they counted, "Twenty, twenty-one, twenty-two . . ."

I had twelve! Twelve measly little drawers, including the ones in the kitchen! No wonder stuff was left out! There just weren't enough places to put all of it.

You would think I would have awakened to that fact without taking a survey, wouldn't you? But that is the way of hidden hindrances. They are not obvious to us until, somehow, we have an "aha" moment.

You'll move forward more efficiently, too, if you zap these hidden hindrances that probably have been slowing you down:

> We shape our dwellings, and afterwards our dwellings shape us.
>
> Winston Churchill

- *Inconvenient work spaces.* Subconsciously, you may put off tasks like paying bills or filling out important forms because you haven't set up a good place to do the job. Make sure you have enough light and the supplies you need are within reach. For instance, if you're paying bills the old-fashioned way, you need stamps, envelopes, pens, and a specific place to stash bills in an organized way.

- *Dressing late in the day.* If late in the day you're still in nightclothes or house slippers, you can't zip the garbage out, take a load to the compost pile, or even step out and soak up some sunshine to brighten your mood. Being fully dressed and wearing street shoes will give you the power to move forward with jobs when they need doing. You'll feel more energized too. Hint: Dressing well and making up the bed are the first two "power actions" of the day.

- *Inadequate storage spaces.* No wonder stuff is sitting around the house! There's no place to put it. But you can solve this problem—either obtain more storage containers or get rid of things you don't need or use. Better yet, do a combination of both! I can assure you, I bought furniture with drawers to make up for *my* deficit.

- *Ugly house.* A beautiful home makes housework meaningful. Few people are enthusiastic about cleaning and organizing an unattractive house. Making your house look more pleasing will add the spark plug you need to your organizational engine. Hint: If you resist spending money

Being fully dressed and wearing street shoes will give you the power to move forward with jobs when they need doing.

on your home, consider the value of investing in a charming place to live. The payoff will be that you are inspired to maintain the loveliness, and inspiration is a powerful motivator.

• *Saboteurs.* Are others making a mess of your home and leaving the work of cleaning up to you? If you're tolerating their bad behavior, yours needs to change too. Retraining them will be easier than you think. My books *When You Live with a Messie* and *Neat Mom, Messie Kids* can help. For details, log on to www.messies.com.

• *Reluctance to accept help.* In some parts of the country, it seems an adult woman would no more think of having someone help with housework than ask for help cutting up the food on her plate. In other areas, hiring household help is common. But even there, some women don't get help because they're perfection driven, embarrassed, or fearful of theft or breakage.

Say What?

One man questioned my advice about getting help, scornfully saying, "Isn't that cheating?" He missed the point. When it comes to getting control of our lives, we're not playing a game; we're accomplishing a goal.

It is my contention that women try to "go it alone" too much of the time. Historically, women have lived and worked in bonding groups. In today's world we no longer gather around the well to get water or at the river to pound our clothes clean, while we talk together, sing, share our needs, and, in general, form a community in which women care about each other and know each other well enough to know how to offer support. Air-conditioning, washing machines and dryers, and the moving cage called a car keep us well isolated from others, unless we take the initiative and set up networks, both social and practical. Start making a list of outside help you may wish to call on for assistance.

My friend Marion, a single working mom, has a bank of "helpers" in her mind and phone book. She considers it one of her gifts to find out what people do well and what they enjoy doing, whether as a business or personal favor. She has a floating mental bank of possibilities if she needs something.

Cut the Stress!

Psychologists have done studies that indicate that having a companion reduces stress. So just making an appointment to get together with someone to do a cleanup job can cement your resolve to actually tackle it—and make you feel better immediately.

- Frank has a truck and picks up or delivers large objects. He's happy to help her when needed.

- Fashion-plate friend Jenny, at Marion's request, comes over and advises her on how to match her clothes fashionably. Marion shares one of her talents with Jenny to return the favor.

- Household help comes to her house from time to time to clean.

- So-and-so paints and another is good at laying tile. She calls on them when necessary.

The point is, Marion knows that even the Lone Ranger needed Tonto—and he didn't lead a very complex life, like we do.

When I talk to people who are struggling alone with an organizational issue, I find that, although they may not have considered it before, with thought, they can recall a friend, family member, or service person who might be just right to hire or ask for help. With my "permission" to go that route, they move forward to success.

Day 34

Upgrade Your House

Without our realizing it, things drift into shabbiness, or at least cease to look their best. Look around. Are there areas in your house that need upgrading so that they contribute to a more gracious way of life?

Consider whether you would be more enthusiastic about your house if you simply spruced up your

- *Flatware.* Are you using bits and pieces of sets in a myriad of styles? Buy a new matching set and enjoy the benefits of being proud of how your table looks. Over the years pieces get nicked in the electric disposal, become dulled with use, and look generally dingy. Certainly, if you are going to entertain, you will do so more happily with a presentable table.

  I'd been shopping for a new set of flatware for a while, and I stumbled upon a set at a discount store for a good price. I said, "Enough with using junky flatware!" and snapped it up. I don't know of any purchase I have en-

> **Without our realizing it, things drift into shabbiness, or at least cease to look their best.**

joyed using quite so much. I hadn't realized how ready for retirement my old set was, until I employed the new one.

- *Shoe area.* Are your shoes lying around in a jumbled pile, kicking at each other in the bottom of your closet? You'll feel better about the entire area if you buy a shoe holder and vacuum the bottom of your closet. Then, and this is very important, get rid of shoes you don't wear. Can't stand throwing them out? Move them into the lives of other people who can happily wear them, while you happily stop storing them. Or throw them away. It's okay. Really. I promise.

- *Towels and sheets.* Are many of yours frayed and grungy? Discard them or use them for rags, and get new ones. But choose towels wisely, depending on your climate and your laundry equipment. I live in hot, humid south Florida, and we use air-conditioning—but only in the

Add a Plant!

Not only can houseplants be a pretty upgrade, they're good for you too! Scientists have found them to be surprisingly efficient at absorbing potentially harmful gases and cleaning the air inside buildings.

middle of summer. I also use a solar dryer (translation: a clothesline), so for me, thin, inexpensive towels are best because they dry faster, both after use and on the line. Also they take up less room in the hamper and on the shelf. Besides, I happen to like them better than heavy towels. For guests, I have a nicer set.

You may love heavy towels and have no problem with washing, drying, and storing big ones. As we all use towels every day, it's important to buy the kind that works for us. In this decision, cost should take a backseat.

It's the same with sheets. You use them nightly, and they meet a very personal need for comfort. So buy what you really like and need. Because sheets last a long time, it helps if you consider that their cost can be spread over an extended period.

Choose a Shoes Solution

If your shoes are jumbled or hard to get to, they are telling you that *you* need to take control. Of the many options, consider which solution fits your needs and your pocketbook: stacking wire racks, shelves, pocketed holders on the backs of closet doors, under-the-bed shoe storage, stacking shoe boxes. You have to decide which method works for you.

I was once surprised when someone asked, "Of course, you keep your shoes on the upper shelves of your closet, don't you?" I didn't, but when I tried it, I found it was an excellent solution for me. My four-year-old granddaughter, on the other hand, keeps hers in the bottom drawer of her dresser. And that's the perfect solution for her.

- *Kitchen cabinets and drawers.* New handles and knobs are inexpensive but will spruce up your kitchen and give lots of bang for the buck. Your local variety store, hardware store, and home store probably have them. Right now give your kitchen hardware an unbiased exam. They may be whispering, "Change me!" If you're not sure, bring home a couple of samples you can return later and hold them up to the cabinet. That should give you a good idea about what you should do.

- *Front door.* It creates a powerful first impression about your house. What does yours say? Does it need repainting? Cleaning? New hardware, such as an updated knob? Would a new seasonal wreath, kick plate, knocker, or some other decoration give it some needed oomph? Do your street numbers and front porch light need refreshing?

- *Storage spaces.* Are you storing things you no longer need or want? Are you storing your grown children's belongings or other people's things? Free up your house by sending these back to their rightful owners. Invest in adequate storage containers for your own things.

- *Rooms.* Has the dining room become a home office? Has the guest room become a storage room? With thought, you may be able to reclaim them for their original purpose, so you can enjoy them more.

- *Flower arrangements and plants.* Are your artificial ones dusty and droopy? Clean them with an air blower or silk flower-cleaning spray. Are your live plants straggly? Repot them or replace them. In the beautiful rooms of decoration magazines, flowers and plants play an important part in making the room come alive. If you imagine those pictures without plants, you will notice the rooms lose a lot of sparkle.

Live your life so you will never have to say, if only.

- *Decorations.* Have too many unplanned items somehow crept onto your shelves? Maybe they're from another era of your life. Maybe they were gifts that no longer "fit" (maybe never did!). Give away, pack away, throw away those that are there because you sort of forgot about them. Try to concentrate on each area where you have decorations with the eyes of a stranger. I'll say it again—use an empty toilet roll or make your hand into a spyglass to see with "new" eyes the areas you suspect might not look their best anymore.

> The home should be an island of sanity in a crazy world.

If all this seems like too much to tackle at once, take a deep breath. Instead of getting overwhelmed, start a list of the areas in your house you've been tolerating but not really enjoying. Then commit to taking steps to upgrade them, one at a time, checking them off your list as you go.

Pretend you're moving and want to make a great impression on the new buyer. Better yet, pretend *you're* the buyer. How does it look? What would make you fall in love with the house? Then upgrade your house for the deserving new owner—you! You'll feel more confident when having people in. And that, in turn, will improve your relationships with others. You'll also find that your energy level and (may I say it) joy will spike as you upgrade what some people call "your larger self"—your home.

> Twenty years from now, you will be more disappointed by the things you didn't do than by the ones you did do. So throw off bow lines. Sail away from the safe harbor. Catch the trade winds in your sails. Explore, dream, discover!
>
> Mark Twain

Day 35

Empty the Area to Be Organized

Want to know a trick to organizing efficiently? Totally clear the area before you begin. Use this method for small jobs, like straightening a closet or bathroom cabinet. Try it for a larger area, like a room or storage area. It's a powerful method.

This method can be time-consuming, however, if the area is large. So budget time to do the job right. It helps to be sure you have enough time, helpers, and storage equipment before you begin. Then thoroughly organize a

- *Room.* First, remove everything from the room. They do that on organizing makeover programs, because it can help you visualize the possibilities of the space with a fresh perspective.

    As you empty the room, possibly out into the yard (assuming you are not doing this in December in Minnesota), deposit each item into one of four zones: *throw away, give away, store elsewhere, return to the room.* Deciding what to return to the room, once it's already out, is much, much easier than deciding what to discard while it's still in place. Tip: If you'd like to paint the room or give it a thorough cleaning, now is the time!

- *Clothes closet.* Once you've removed all of the clothes and things kept on the shelves of your closet, surely you won't put back things you have not worn in a year (or is that years?), things that don't match anything, things that don't fit, and things you don't like. Consider painting the closet white, before you fill it again, so it won't need to be painted each time the color of the room is changed. What a future time-saver!

- *Car trunk.* Whether you clean it yourself or have the job done by a professional, while the items are out, evaluate what you want to discard, store elsewhere, or return to the trunk. Get rid of the excess. And consider adding some appropriately sized storage containers to keep organized the things you plan to return to the trunk.

- *China cabinet.* Without your careful design, a lot of knick-knacks tend to find a home here. Someone's gift, a family picture, an impulse buy of something "cute." They all stand side by side, full of memories but lacking style.

  To remedy the situation, totally empty the cabinet. Then return only the items you really like—

and the ones that look good there. Observe the newly decorated cabinet with an objective eye. Evaluate whether you need to buy anything for the unused spaces, or use those areas to display items you have elsewhere in the house.

Put items you don't return to the china cabinet in storage boxes. Save the boxed excess in an out-of-the-way place. Now, light up your china cabinet with confidence that it will reflect beauty within your home. (If your china cabinet has closed glass doors, they save oodles of time in dusting.)

- *Storage closet, storage room, attic, or garage.* These areas often are stuffed with miscellaneous items and junk, so before you begin, be sure you have time to finish the whole job.

  As you empty the storage area, group like items. Put everything that's going back into the area in an appropriate container, and boldly label the outside of each.

  Keep the floor of the area as clear as possible by hanging bulky items, such as brooms and large tools, on the wall or from an out-of-the-way beam. Then they will be easier to see and retrieve.

  Be sure you're properly prepared with enough storage boxes, garbage containers, shelving, hooks for hanging, even a rented Dumpster, if necessary. Have enough help, either volunteer or hired. And, if needed, rent or borrow a pickup truck. Some people find that renting a portable temporary storage unit, like those from PODS, lessens the stress, because you don't have to finish the job in just one day or weekend.

When you clear any area, and see before you an empty space, you'll probably feel a surge of enthusiasm to do the job—and do it right! When the junk is separated and discarded and the "keepers" are finally stored and clearly labeled, you'll feel like a million bucks. You had to invest a lot of time, energy, and (let's face it) stress in getting it done, but once it's organized, it will be well worth the effort. You've made an investment in a stress-free future.

Day 36

Revamp Your Family Room and Kitchen

It's time. You can avoid it no longer. You're now ready to attack your rooms, one by one, giving them your full attention, until they're organized and can be maintained in a smooth-running process that's far easier than you ever imagined.

First, schedule a time to work on each room. Then plan your attack. For each room, you'll need to

- *Take inventory.* How much do you need to store? Buy storage containers only *after* you've determined the groups of like items that will be stored together. That will ensure you buy the right containers for the job. Avoid using very large bins for lots of small items—they're easy to fill, but it's hard to find and retrieve the small items when needed. Large bins can be used to hold a few bulky items.
- *Note places that attract clutter,* such as near the door or by the bed. Rather than try to break the habit of storing things

there, go with it. Just find attractive storage containers that can keep items that land there organized and uncluttered.

- *Identify things that can be hung*—and hang anything you can. Most homes have much more free vertical than horizontal space. And hanging things keeps the floor clear and makes quick cleanups far easier. Revel in brooms and mops neatly suspended in the utility closet; pans aligned on a kitchen wall, rather than in a jumble in the cupboard; tools hung where you can easily find them in the garage; sporting equipment at an easy-to-reach height in a child's room, rather than in a pile on the closet floor.

- *Take lighting seriously,* placing lights (either electric or battery operated) in closets, where you read, and in any murky spots where you find yourself squinting or straining to see.

- *Compress what you can* in plastic storage bags that expel air, squeezing clothes and other items flat. Some of these plastic bags are made to be used with a vacuum to suck the air out. You can use a vacuum hose to do the same with regular trash bags closed tightly with rubber bands. With others, you can displace the air manually. An amazing amount of things take up little space when the air is removed. Hint: Be sure to open the bags after about six months to fluff stored items, if necessary. Schedule it on your calendar, so you don't forget!

- *Stow extra pillows, blankets, or other bulky items* in a tall trash can, covered with a round top and round tablecloth designed to fit. You have created a decorative table with hidden storage on which you may place a lamp or flowers.

Now it's time to take action. Let's tackle these areas together.

Free the Family Room

If you are cramped for space, as many of us are, it may help to

- *Create space-saving end tables* by placing decorative filing cabinets at each end of the sofa. Inside, stow bills, banking information, craft and office supplies, and other miscellaneous items that you use in that area. You could give plain cabinets a decorative touch by covering them with a tablecloth. When you need to get into one of the drawers, just flip up the cloth.
- *To save space, use swing-arm lamps that mount on the wall,* instead of floor lamps or tabletop models.
- *Use the back of the door for storage.* Organizing stores and catalogs offer an array of hooks, holders, racks, baskets, pockets, and the like for storage overflow. You can find hanging holders for files (I have one on the back of my home office door), for DVDs or cassettes, coats, shoes, children's toys, and many other items. Just be sure these hanging storage areas don't end up being unsightly.
- *Think storage,* when it's time to buy more furniture. For instance, buy an ottoman with a storage compartment inside or a TV stand with drawers or cabinet space.

- *Slide flat items out of sight.* For example, folding chairs you use only occasionally and TV trays may fit nicely behind or under the sofa or bed.

Conquer the Kitchen

An easy-to-use, organized kitchen is within reach. Really! The key is so simple—smart storage. Try these tips:

- *Group like items together* for easy access when working. Keep often used items within arm's reach, tucking away seldom used items in more out-of-the-way locations.
- *Keep things close to where you use them most.* For example, keep pots and pans within easy reach of the stove. Cluster dishes and eating utensils near the dishwasher and sink for easier cleanup. It's a simple principle, but one that's often violated.
- *Have a step stool close by.* Even when you've stored things as conveniently as possible, some things will still be hard to reach. A stool that folds and slides into a narrow space is the best choice. If you are buying one, do yourself a favor and get one with two steps. You will be glad you did—probably sooner than you imagine.
- *Bring the back forward.* The deepest part of cabinets becomes easily accessible with the installation of inexpensive, wire drawers or a lazy Susan. There are even slide-out bins configured to fit around under-sink pipes. And more recently on the market, there are slide-out trays designed for the refrigerator.
- *Don't buy in bulk,* unless you know you have ample convenient places to store what you buy.

- *Install a flip-out storage tray under the panel in front of your kitchen sink.* They're great for holding sponges, vegetable scrubbers and other small, around-the-sink items. I found a kit at my local home store, near the cabinet department. It was about the price of a meal at a midlevel restaurant, which is to say, pretty inexpensive. If you can use a screwdriver, you should be able to install it yourself—at least that's what the salesman said.

- *De-jumble with vinyl-coated wire organizers.* Use them for pot lids, platters, place mats, whatever. There are models that sit on shelves, mount to the wall or cabinet, or install as slide-out drawers.

- *Hang cooking utensils* above the countertop, near the stove. They'll be easier to reach, and you'll free up valuable drawer and cabinet space. This works for pots too!

- *Store seldom used equipment elsewhere.* The turkey roaster you use once a year won't mind being relocated to a storage closet, the garage, or the basement. Worried you won't remember where you put it? Post a note to yourself inside a cabinet door.

- *Add instant shelving.* Put inexpensive wire or plastic shelves on legs into cabinets to double shelf space.

- *Think up, up, up.* In the kitchen too there's usually more vertical space than horizontal. So stack lids and baking dishes. Hang knives and other metal utensils on a magnetic bar attached to the cabinet or wall. Use a Peg-Board for hanging items if drawers are overflowing.

- *Put under-cabinet space to work.* For example, add a narrow shelf between cabinets and countertop to hold small, often used items, such as spices. As you replace worn-out appliances, consider space-saving models that mount under cabinets.

- *Build a shelf about a foot below the ceiling* around the kitchen walls. Store seldom used items there in decorative baskets and containers.
- *Buy a portable dishwasher* that rolls to the sink when you need it if you don't have a built-in model. The top provides additional space for food preparation.
- *Designate zones in the refrigerator.* For example, keep all cheeses in one place, all condiments in another. Place as many things as possible in door shelves, where they're easily accessible. Attach labels to remind you—and others.
- *Meander around display kitchens* at a home store. You'll be inspired to adapt their best ideas to your own spaces.

Now enjoy the fruits of your labor. Your house is really becoming the ultracomfortable, organized retreat of your dreams.

Day 37

Revamp Your Laundry, Closets, Bedrooms, and Bathrooms

Okay, ready to make progress in other areas of the house? With no further ado, let's get to it.

Lay Out Your Laundry Area

You'll gain valuable space and a decluttered look if you

- *Smartly store your ironing board.* Hang it on an over-the-door ironing board hook, found at home supply stores. Or buy an ironing board that mounts on the wall and folds down. Store the iron within reach. Hint: If you don't do much ironing, or if you do a lot of quick touch-ups, buy a small board. One kind sits on a table or counter.

The best kind fits over an extended drawer and hooks under the counter, allowing clothes to hang as you iron. Both models are easy to store and retrieve.

> Obstacles are those things we notice when we take our eyes off our goal.
>
> Henry Ford

- *Keep a trash can close* to the dryer for lint and the debris you find in pockets. Also keep a cup or jar handy for money and other good items left in the pockets.
- *Install a shelf for laundry supplies* above the washer and dryer. Add a space for hanging clothes by installing a tension rod designed for shower curtains.
- *Add a slim storage unit* on wheels, between the washer and dryer. This is available in many catalogs and home stores.

Cure Clothes Closet Blues

Just dive in and

- *Give clothes a deadline.* Those you're not using need to go elsewhere, either into storage, into a bin to be given away, or into the garbage. To determine which clothes aren't getting worn enough to justify the closet space they take, turn all of the hangers so that the end of the hook points toward you. Each time you wear a piece of clothing, hang it with the hook facing the back of the closet. Place a note reminding yourself of when you began this clothes evaluation project. At the end of a year (or sooner) move the clothes on hangers that are still turned outward, because they have not been worn, to a home where they are more needed and appreciated, preferably the nearest charity.

- *Replace wire hangers with good quality plastic—in one color.* Plastic hangers hang more neatly and using just one color makes the closet look more orderly. Buy some with clamps to hold skirts and slacks. Keep clothespins close by to secure garments that tend to slip off their hangers.

- *Place a shelf just above the closet door, on the inside.* Stow seldom used or seasonal items there.

- *Paint the closet walls white,* if they're not already. White reflects more light, brightening the space and making it easier to see what you need. And when the walls are white, you won't need to repaint every time you change the color of the outer room's walls.

Beautify Your Bedroom

It's important to avoid allowing the bedroom to become an overflow for the home office, sewing room, or any other

One Person's Reflection on Organizing Dresser Drawers

I could never keep my (or my husband's) drawers straight. So I came up with this mental plan: undershirts and bras in the top drawers, panties and boxers in the middle, socks and stockings in the bottom! I just have to picture a body and I know where stuff goes! Just a hint! Hope it works for you!

A Reforming Messie

space. This is your personal sanctuary and should be protected from intrusions that will disturb the peace you find there.

With careful planning, the bedroom can serve many purposes, without disrupting the ambience. The secret is to use maximum wall space and minimal floor space. Ideally the room should have a floor-to-ceiling storage unit with drawers and shelves to hold a myriad of belongings.

Until you can afford to add a unit like that, take advantage of hidden spaces with storage potential, like under the bed. Long, shallow, plastic containers with wheels are designed for this. You'll gain even more space by slightly elevating the bed with a set of bed-risers. They come in sizes from three to twelve inches. The ones I have are six inches high. You might also consider buying—or building—a bed platform, with built-in drawers.

To have a bathroom that consistently looks well kept, you must commit to two good habits—always returning what is used to the proper spot and always wiping spills immediately.

Better Your Bathroom

To have a bathroom that consistently looks well kept, you must commit to two good habits—always returning what is used to the proper spot and always wiping spills immediately.

To set up a well-organized bathroom, simply

- Create enough hanging space for towels.
- Use the space above the toilet for an added cabinet or shelves.

- Remove medicines from the "medicine" cabinet. Bathrooms are too moist and warm to store them safely. Instead, put them in sealed plastic containers in a cooler, drier place.
- Store children's bath toys in a caddy that can be mounted to the tub wall with suction cups.
- Install wall-mounted holders for items like toothbrushes, razors, soap dishes, and more. This makes cleaning a snap.
- Add a plastic shoe holder to the back of a door to hold small items.
- Add space for towels by installing swinging towel bars that attach to, and are supported by, the door hinge. A company called Hinge-It makes and sells these unique towel holders that hide behind the bathroom door. Adults hang their towels on the top hinge. Children can reach those mounted on a lower hinge. As always, make it easy for kids to cooperate.
- Install slide-out vinyl-wire drawers on the floor of the sink cabinets so you can pull items forward for easy reach.
- Keep kids' grooming products in a basket or bucket that can be stored in their rooms when they're not being used in the bathroom. This reduces clutter—and prevents squabbles!

By now, half of your house has been transformed. Stick to it! You're almost there!

Revamp Your Kids' Rooms, Garage, Attic, Basement, and Home Office

Look at the progress you've made! Look around. You're gaining control. I'm proud of you, and happy for you too.

But this is no time to rest on our laurels. Let's just get right back at it.

Conquer Chaos in Kids' Rooms

A few children are naturally predisposed to order. Most are not. Often messy children's rooms trigger family conflict, but it doesn't have to be that way.

Children can learn not only to maintain an organized room but also to enjoy it. If you make it easy for children to keep their rooms neat, you'll decrease conflict in your home while

If you make it easy for children to keep their rooms neat, you'll decrease conflict in your home.

they're living there, and increase the chance they'll be organized adults when they're grown and gone. You'll be on the right path if you

- *Establish zones* for grooming, play, dressing, and study. Then group the items that fit into each zone. Learning to group like items is an intellectual pursuit that will benefit your children organizationally for the rest of their lives.
- *Label the zones* with words—pictures for nonreaders—to remind them which things should be stored there.
- *Remember, kids are short.* Make sure shelves, drawers, and closet hangers are low enough for them to use. Make sure drawer handles are large enough for them to grasp, and make sure drawers slide easily.
- *Visit a school supply store* for ideas. There are many tools for neatly organizing kid-size things.
- *Shun large toy boxes,* except to contain very large toys. Small toys or toy pieces will get lost at the bottom. Place toys neatly in clear, plastic boxes with labels. Or add a plastic shoe holder with pockets to the back of a door—it's a great tool for storing small things.
- *Decorate in a way that excites children.* They'll be much more enthusiastic about keeping rooms neat and showing them off.
- *Show—don't just tell.* Your children learn by watching your habits. With your consistent guidance, they'll pick up good habits too and will be more likely to make good use of the well-organized rooms you've created for them.
- *Keep short accounts.* Remind children to put items back where they belong on a regular basis.

Groom the Garage

A two-car garage covers about five hundred square feet of floor space. That's about the size of a small apartment!

Two parked cars take up half the space in the garage, when you include room for the car doors to open. This leaves a significant amount of room for storage, and (drumroll, please!) it's the best kind because most is along the walls. To make the most of it

- *Designate zones,* as in other rooms. You may have a building zone for storage of hammers, drills, wrenches, and the like. The garden/lawn zone would include tools hung from hooks on the wall. Sports equipment often fits nicely in a wheeled trash can—labeled, of course—in the sports zone. If you use the garage for general storage for things like games, dog food, decorations, and more, create zones for each category and post signs labeling each zone. That will nudge you—and other family members—to take that extra step and put things away properly after use. Hint: Arrange zones so that items used frequently are near the garage door you use most.

- *Measure spaces carefully* before buying storage containers.

- *Keep things off the floor.* You can hang things for pennies if you hammer large nails into studs around the walls. Peg-Boards keep smaller items neat. Putting things away is a snap if you trace around them, leaving an outline that shows where they should be returned after use. Anything that can't hang should be in labeled

> It never occurred to me until I had this house to take a vacation and stay home.
>
> Gill Robinson, decorator

containers, stored neatly on shelves. Lightweight items can go on high shelves; heavy items should stay low. If you can afford them, cabinets with doors create a neater overall look.

- *Put rafters to work.* Exposed rafters can hold a multitude of items. Slide skis and ski poles, long and thin sports equipment, even long gardening tools onto a ladder hung horizontally from the ceiling, above your head but within reach. Suspend large tools and sports equipment—especially bicycles—from hooks screwed into the rafters.

- *Make it shine.* As you organize, give the garage a good cleaning, discarding things you haven't used in years. It doesn't have to be spotless. But the neater it is, the more likely you'll be to keep it that way. Hint: Make oil stains fade by using your foot to grind unused kitty litter into the greasy spot. After a few hours, sweep up the litter with the oil it has absorbed. Prevent future stains by taping a piece of cardboard over the spot where you

When All Else Fails

In her book *Conquering Chronic Disorganization*, Judith Kolberg describes using pulleys in a client's garage to hoist a fishing net full of clutter up twelve feet to the top. The client simply couldn't categorize those items to organize them, so he settled on lowering the net occasionally and rummaging through it for what he needed. Quirky and a little impractical but interesting and useful in the long run.

normally park. When you want to spruce up, simply change the cardboard for a new piece.

Warning: Use only the area around the perimeter of the garage for storage. Don't be sucked into using the middle. Just because the space is there doesn't mean it should be used. You'll be far more comfortable and satisfied pulling your car into a well-cleared garage.

> Your home functions like a small business, so develop an office space that will help you manage your home in an organized way.

Attend to the Attic and Basement

Often attics and basements are untapped resources that can take a lot of clutter-pressure off the rest of the house. If these areas are unfinished, only durable items can be stored there. Moisture can ruin clothing and fragile items, unless they're stored in airtight containers. And even then, temperature extremes can be damaging.

However, if you paint walls and floors with a product that seals and waterproofs, you'll give items stored there more protection, and the area will be more attractive. With a coat of bright paint and plenty of lighting, an attic or basement can be an inviting laundry center, home office, workshop, or craft room. And it will lure you to return items more consistently to their proper places.

In both areas, follow the "rules" of storage. Designate zones, label each zone with a sign, and group like items in labeled containers. Make a master list of the contents of each box, and leave it near the entrance.

> Your house is your larger self.

Organize a Home Office

Your home functions like a small business, so it's important to develop an office space that will help you manage your home in an organized way. You may need only a small area for record keeping and bill paying. If you conduct outside business from your home, you'll need a larger area.

Where will this be? you ask. Consider a spare bedroom, a basement, even a closet. Computer armoires that can hold a compact office, when closed, can blend with the décor of nearly any room without looking out of place. And the contents are completely hidden!

Some people don't need a desk. They work fine at a table, when necessary, and can keep everything they need stored in one place in a box or filing system.

For any home office two tools are indispensable in cutting paper clutter—a computer and a wastebasket. A filing system is nearly as important.

Well, you've done it. You've organized your home. Look around. Don't you love it? Congratulations on a job well done!

Day  39

Control Your Time

You've gotten your house nicely organized and you've developed habits to keep it that way. Good for you! One more thing is necessary for an organized life—learning to control how you use your time.

It's not hard, once you know how. Organized people understand the two secrets that make it easy and guarantee success. They focus on priorities and divvy up their time wisely to reach them.

That means, you simply must:

- *Say* no *to less-important, C-list priorities.* We have so many opportunities and so many demands on our time in today's busy world. That makes it important to practice saying no to the requests of other people and often to our own desires as well. We don't have the time or the energy to do everything. That means we have to ignore what we may call our C list, in favor of giving our attention to what's essential.

• *Shout a resounding* yes *to a few, well-selected activities in your life—your A-list priorities.* When the yes areas are determined, you can say no more easily to other areas, many of which may be excellent activities, but just are not right for you at this time.

Share the Work—Dele-great!

Create more time for the tasks that really matter by becoming a "greater delegator." To help you in your effort to reassign some of your tasks to others, ask yourself these questions:

- Am I doing jobs that would be more appropriate for others to do?
- Am I still treating my older children as though they are small and need me to do everything for them? (This isn't fair to you or to them.)
- Do I fail to hire outside help because I think I should do it all?
- Am I doing it all to prove I'm needed?
- Do I hate to impose on others?
- Am I not sure how to go about delegating to others?
- Do I feel it's easier to do it myself, rather than supervise others?
- Am I neglecting to train my younger children to be independent and helpful?

If you answered yes to any of these questions, it's time to start asking others to share the load. You may be surprised how happily others go along with the new division of labor. Start today! You'll be glad you did.

- *Determine the difference.* Not clear about what should be on your A list and what should be delegated to your C list? You're not alone, but it's important to get that straight now.

Your A List

You can start determining your A list by simply listing five areas that are priorities in your life and trying to put them in order of importance. One of the priorities must be keeping up with the trivial, routine tasks of housekeeping, because those tasks fit into the larger important context of organization. These five are your A list.

1. routine housekeeping tasks
2.
3.
4.
5.

When it comes to divvying up your time, ask yourself how much you can give to each of your priority areas. It's an important matter to settle now, because you'll need to make sure you're leaving enough time to give adequate attention to all of your A-list priorities. For example, if church work or some other ministry is in your Top Five, you need to decide how much time and energy you can put into that area and still leave enough time for the other four.

> Things which matter most must never be at the mercy of things which matter least.
>
> Johann Wolfgang von Goethe, nineteenth-century poet

Your B List

Put important tasks that are not your top priority but need to be done on a B list.

    1.

    2.

    3.

Your C List

You have already chosen your A and B lists. Can you determine one or two time-consuming items that are basically unproductive in your life and (gasp!) able to be tossed? Now, commit to tossing them!

    1.

    2.

Day 40

Bonus Maintenance Program

You've got disorganization on the run! You're probably eager to keep moving forward in your organizational life without slipping back. Well, you *can* by using this simple and fun six-week maintenance program. (Hint: For maximum effect, enlist your whole family!)

Here's how this maintenance program works.

First, read the following suggestions for each week. Choose two you haven't yet put in place in your organizational plan and commit to them.

Some will be exceedingly simple for you. Others will take more effort. Some require only a little thinking and planning. Others are action-oriented. Some will be onetime tasks. Others will be habits you'll want to put into place for good. Choose what *you* want to tackle.

Like the changes you put in place during the preceding chapters, this maintenance plan is designed as a series of

Like the changes you put in place during the preceding chapters, this maintenance plan is designed as a series of small, manageable steps.

small, manageable steps. Just start poking holes in a project. Enough holes, and the project is done.

With each of the activities listed below, you'll move one step (or hole) closer to developing and maintaining your own organized home. So for each week, check the two activities that appeal to you, then commit. Maybe you'll want to give a copy of the list to each member of your family, so they can choose their own tasks as well. You can download and print copies from www.messies.com. Post the list in a visible place, like on the refrigerator, so you won't forget your commitment.

Now let's begin!

Six Weeks to an (Even More!) Organized Life

Week One

___ Make your bed every day for one week.

___ Try a new cleaning product—for the oven, carpet, bathroom, anywhere.

___ Determine a problem area, either a perpetually disorganized place in your home, such as a jumbled vanity drawer or a child's room; or a habit that causes disarray, like dropping books at the door. Focus on the problem and write it down.

___ Devise a workable solution for a problem area.

___ Straighten up the house for fifteen minutes before bed every evening.

___ Organize a drawer.

___ Discard an unused toy and/or kitchen gadget.

___ Clear and organize the kitchen counter.

___ Write out a simple household-maintenance schedule.

___ Write several motivational mottos and post them where you will see them often.

Week Two

___ Peruse cleaning products at the store, reading their labels to discover new products that can reduce your

Eye, Eye!

A patch may be an impressive accessory for a pirate, but to avoid having to wear one because of an eye infection, the experts at the U.S. Food and Drug Administration say you should:

- **Discard any eye-area cosmetics you've had longer than three months, especially mascara.**
- **Toss out cosmetics that have hardened or dried out, even if they're nearly new. Adding water or saliva to moisten them introduces bacteria that could harm your eyes.**
- **If you've had an eye infection, get rid of all eye-area products you were using at the time, including applicators. They may be contaminated.**
- **Be wary of products labeled "all natural." They may have substances that encourage microbial growth, and they may increase the risk of contamination.**

cleaning time. Also seek new uses for products you're already using.

___ Purchase and put into use a new organizing product, such as a shoe rack, drawer divider, or pot-lid hanger.

___ Keep the sink clear of dishes all day for one day.

___ Write a letter to your house telling it what you intend to do for it.

___ Discard at least one outdated periodical, hopefully more.

___ Donate books and/or videos you're not using to the library, your church, or a charity.

___ Finish—or discard!—an unfinished project.

___ Throw out makeup you're not using anymore.

___ Pull unused clothing out of one closet and donate it to charity.

___ Organize a kitchen cabinet.

___ Repeat your favorite motivational mottos aloud several times.

Week Three

___ Develop an organizational plan for the whole family. Delegate chores.

___ Call a family council meeting to discuss your organizational plans.

___ Talk to a significant family member about your organizational goals.

___ Find and display a magazine picture that represents your dream home.

____ Write out five or more dream statements about your house.

____ List your three greatest frustrations about your house.

Cool It!

You've had that thawed meat in the refrigerator for only three days, so it's perfectly safe, right? Not necessarily, say experts at the Food Safety and Inspection Service, part of the U.S. Department of Agriculture. Most uncooked meats can be stored safely in the fridge for just one or two days. After that, it could be dangerous to eat it. That is a good reason to organize your eating plan to keep food moving onto the table while it's fresh.

To keep your family safe, it's better to follow the old adage, When in doubt, throw it out. Here are some guidelines. You can refrigerate

- egg salad, chicken salad, or other prepared salad for three to five days
- cooked ham slices for three to four days
- prestuffed cuts of pork, lamb, or chicken for one day
- opened packages of hot dogs for one week
- opened packages of lunch meat for three to five days
- soups and stews for three to four days
- raw sausage for a day or two
- leftover cooked hamburger patties, poultry, or fish for a day or two
- raw chicken, fish, or shellfish for a day or two

For complete guidelines, log on to www.fsis.usda.gov or call the food-safety hotline at 888-674-6854.

___ Recruit a buddy who will hold you accountable for your progress.

___ Write and post a reminder to family members, and/or yourself, to help keep trouble areas in shape.

___ Throw out old food from the refrigerator.

___ Peruse cleaning tools in the grocery or hardware store.

___ Write a menu for the week and post it on the refrigerator.

___ Log on to www.messies.com, join an online group there, and read postings about others' successes in getting organized.

Week Four

___ Rearrange furniture in one room.

___ Plan a garage sale.

___ Handle all mail appropriately—the day it arrives.

___ Save or print old email you need. Delete the rest.

___ Buy or make a bill organizer, a container that keeps bills nicely organized and handy on a wall or in a drawer.

___ Set up a system to organize your files.

___ Set up a box or boxes to hold decorations for each holiday.

Week Five

___ Discard one thing from your closet.

___ Organize a sewing box, a hobby kit, or craft material.

___ Locate a professional household organizer in your area by logging on to the website of the National Association of Professional Organizers, at www.napo.net.

___ Talk to a professional organizer about his or her services.

How Much Do They Really Help?

In a recent survey, about 25 percent of parents admitted to nagging their children "constantly" about cleaning their rooms. However, American children, ages six to eighteen, contribute about 12 percent of all household labor, Arizona State University family sociologist Sampson Lee Blair has found. Blair found that minority children pitch in more around the house. And for all groups, the more housework Mom does, the more kids help.

Chores are good for kids. Not only does pitching in help the family overall, completing chores helps them learn to assume responsibility, gain autonomy, and get practical life skills, including decision making, before they reach adulthood.

In most American homes, children begin helping with chores around age six, with simple tasks, like picking up toys and taking out trash, Blair says. The older the child, the more complex the task he or she is able to accomplish.

Parents of teens won't be surprised that the number of household chores completed by sixteen- to eighteen-year-olds declines sharply. For more information about how you can rally your family to help, read my book *Neat Mom, Messie Kids.*

___ Develop a chore list and a system of rewarding your children for their regular help.

___ Skip a TV program and organize something instead.

___ Ask friends to recommend a housekeeper or cleaning service.

___ Pretend you are a stranger entering your front door for the first time. Look around to get a fresh view.

___ Discard games and puzzles that have missing pieces or boxes that are tattered beyond reasonable repair.

___ Interview an organized person you admire and ask for tips. Find out if organization came naturally or was learned.

___ Hire a plumber, electrician, or handyman to do a repair job that's been neglected.

Week Six

___ Choose a home-improvement project—and take steps to do it!

___ Clean the car—the inside, the outside, or both—on your own, or by hiring someone.

___ Invite friends over.

___ Throw out all pens and markers that don't work.

___ Throw out all family members who don't work (a little organizational humor)!

___ Visit an automotive store to consider organizational products for the car.

___ Scout out the organizing section of a variety or hardware store for organizing products.

___ Flip through an interior decorating magazine or book for ideas and styles that appeal to you.

_____ Start a home decorating–idea scrapbook or box to keep examples or illustrations of materials and ideas you like. (Hint: Read my book *Living Organized* for specifics on doing this effectively.)

_____ Visit an office supply store for ideas on how to organize, especially papers.

_____ Consolidate and organize snapshots.

Now keep that progress going! Sign up for my daily email message, "The Organizer Lady," on www.messies.com to receive motivation, reminders, and helpful hints. I'm cheering for you. Let's connect every day, so I can remind you that the secret to success is making very small, yet very consistent, changes—baby steps, baby steps in the right direction!

Resources

Books on organizing life fall into several categories. To complement the topics of this book, you may want to look into some of the topics and books below.

If I wanted more information on improving my life organizationally, I would go to my local bookstore and look for books in the household section. The latest books on organizing, including some classics, are nestled among the books on decorating and home repair. Books about taking control of and simplifying one's life are scattered throughout the self-improvement section.

A second place I would look, depending on its proximity, is the local library. It may or may not have the latest books, but it will have books that are no longer on the bookstore shelves. The oldies are often the goodies.

The third place to look is at an online bookstore. Type in the words *household organizing* (if you put in *organizing* alone, you may get information on starting a union) or *simplicity*. Look to see if reviews of books by other readers are available.

I encourage you to refer to my other books, all published by Revell: *The New Messies Manual*—the flagship book for change; *The Messie Motivator*; *Messie No More*; *Neat Mom, Messie Kids*; and *When You Live with a Messie*.

Simplicity

Davidson, Jeff. *Breathing Space: Living and Working at a Comfortable Pace in a Sped-up Society.* New York: MasterMedia Limited, 1991.

Jones, Sheila, ed. *Finding Balance.* Billerica, MA: Discipleship Publications, 2002.

Time Management

Davidson, Jeff. *The Complete Idiot's Guide to Managing Your Time.* New York: Alpha Books, 1995.

Macgee-Cooper, Ann, with Duane Trammell. *Time Management for Unmanageable People.* New York: Bantam, 1994.

Otto, Donna. *Get More Done in Less Time.* Eugene, OR: Harvest House, 1995.

Clutter

Aslett, Don. *Not for Packrats Only: How to Clean Up, Clear Out, and Dejunk Your Life Forever.* New York: Penguin, 1991.

Campbell, Jeff. *Clutter Control: Putting Your Home on a Diet.* New York: Dell, 1992.

Neziroglu, Fugen, Jerome Bubrick, and Tobias Yaryura. *Overcoming Compulsive Hoarding.* Oakland: New Harbinger, 2004.

Organizing

Cilley, Marla. *Sink Reflections.* New York: Bantam, 2002.

Lockwood, Georgene. *The Complete Idiot's Guide to Organizing Your Life.* New York: Alpha Books, 1996.

Mendelson, Cheryl. *Home Comforts: The Art and Science of Keeping House.* New York: Scribner, 1999.

Rich, Jason. *The Everything Organize Your Home Book: Straighten Up the Entire House, from Cleaning Your Closets to Reorganizing Your Kitchen*. Avon, MA: Adams Media, 2002.

Roth, Eileen, with Elizabeth Miles. *Organizing for Dummies*. New York: Hungry Minds, 2002.

Williams, Debbie. *Put Your House in Order: Organizing Strategies Straight from the Word*. Houston: Let's Get It Together, 2002.

Paper Organizing Tips

Barnes, Emilie. *The Fifteen-Minute Organizer*. Eugene, OR: Harvest House, 1991.

Smallin, Donna. *Unclutter Your Home: Seven Simple Steps, Seven Hundred Tips and Ideas*. Pownal, VT: Storey Books, 1999.

Winston, Stephanie. *Best Organizing Tips*. New York: Simon and Schuster, 1996.

Parenting

Elkind, David. *The Hurried Child: Growing Up Too Fast Too Soon*. Cambridge, MA: Perseus, 2001.

Felton, Sandra. *Neat Mom, Messie Kids*. Grand Rapids: Revell, 2002.

Rosenfield, Alvin, and Nicole Wise. *The Over-Scheduled Child: Avoiding the Hyper-Parenting Trap*. New York: St. Martin's, 2000.

Tinglof, Christina Baglivi. *The Organized Parent: Three Hundred Sixty-Five Simple Solutions to Managing Your Home, Your Time, and Your Family's Life*. New York: Contemporary Books, 2002.

Websites about Organizing

Websites have a limited life, but by using a search engine, you will be able to find many that can help.

www.messies.com—The website of Messies Anonymous, founded by Sandra Felton. Contains a lot of information for those who struggle with disorder in their lives. Join online groups for regular support in making changes.

http://groups.yahoo.com/group/The-Organizer-Lady—Sign up for daily encouragement and reminders from Sandra Felton to keep on track and in focus.

www.OnlineOrganizing.com—"A world of organizing solutions." Read excellent articles, join discussion groups, get questions answered by professional organizers.

www.OrganizersWebRing.com—Professional Organizers Web Ring or POWR. Their motto is "You've got the POWR to get organized." Find a professional organizer in your area and read articles on many subjects that affect your everyday organizing life.

www.nsgcd.org—National Study Group on Chronic Disorganization. "The premier online resource for anyone interested (personally or professionally) in Chronic Disorganization."

www.napo.net—National Association of Professional Organizers. Locate a professional organizer in your area or learn how to become one.

www.faithfulorganizers.com—This is a website for Christian Professional Organizers. It is the only place where faith and professional organizing meet. This site helps people all over the country locate professional organizers in their area who also share their values. They are a resource for churches to find speakers for their women's groups and moms' groups.

Catalogs for Organizing

The Container Store catalog at www.containerstore.com or 800-733-3532. They offer many organizing solutions for the home or office, including closet design, with free personalized planning service in the stores, over the phone, and online.

Get Organized catalog at www.shopgetorganized.com or 800-803-9400. Check out their many "space-saving innovations to unclutter your life."

Hold Everything catalog at www.holdeverything.com is a catalog of storage and household ideas from Williams-Sonoma.

Lillian Vernon catalogs at www.lillianvernon.com or 800-545-5426. Their household organizing catalogs *Neat Ideas* emphasize decorative organizers and tools for every room in the house.

Organize-Everything catalog at www.organize-everything.com has clothing storage items.

Organize It catalog at www.organize-it.com has lots of clothing storage products.

The Storage Store at www.thestoragestore.com has a nice variety of storage boxes.

Catalogs for Cleaning

Clean Report, from Don Aslett, America's Number One Source for Cleaning Information at www.cleanreport.com or 800-451-2402. Don has available many books and videos on cleaning as well as cleaning tools and products.

Home Improvements: Hundreds of Quick and Clever Problem-Solvers! at www.improvementscatalog.com or 800-642-2112 has lots of interesting things for use around the home, including many unique organizing products.

Home Trends at www.hometrendscatalog.com or 800-810-2340. This catalog emphasizes cleaning products but offers organizing products as well.

High- and Low-Tech Cleaning Schedule Resources

The Flipper is a system of organizing cleaning jobs available from *Messies Anonymous*. For information: www.messies.com or check how you can make your own in *The New Messies Manual* or *The Messies Superguide*.

The Internet has several cleaning schedule lists available online from various groups. A recent search on Google under "household cleaning schedule" turned up 5621 links, several of which looked excellent.

Create your own daily schedule using your computer calendar or online reminders, which may come with your provider service.

Online Cooking Resources

Type *recipes* in your search engine, and your poor little computer will sag with the weight of the responses.

Check out www.30daygourmet.com for cook and freeze suggestions.

Filing Resources

Hemphill, Barbara. *Taming the Paper Tiger at Home.* Washington, D.C.: Kiplinger, 2002.

Sandra Felton, The Organizer Lady™, is the author of many books on bringing order and beauty to the home, including the best-selling *The Messies Manual* and *Messie No More*. She is founder and president of Messies Anonymous, a group for those who seek a new and better way of life. Through her encouragement and information, many have found relief and brought organization and harmony to their lives, homes, and family life. For more information, log on to www.messies.com.

Sandra speaks at women's conferences and is a frequent guest on national radio and TV shows. She lives with her husband in Miami, Florida.